Wild Goose big book *of* worship resources 2

Wild Goose big book of worship resources 2

wild goose
publications
www.ionabooks.com

Contributions copyright © the individual contributors
Compilation © The Iona Community
Published 2019 by
Wild Goose Publications
21 Carlton Court, Glasgow G5 9JP, UK,
the publishing division of the Iona Community.
Scottish Charity No. SC003794. Limited Company Reg. No. SC096243.

ISBN 978-1-84952-684-5

Cover photo © Mikko Pitkänen / Alias Studiot Oy | Dreamstime.com

The publishers gratefully acknowledge the support of the Drummond Trust, 3 Pitt Terrace, Stirling FK8 2EY in producing this book.

All rights reserved. Apart from the circumstances described below relating to non-commercial use, no part of this publication may be reproduced in any form or by any means, including photocopying or any information storage or retrieval system, without written permission from the publisher.

Non-commercial use: The material in this book may be used non-commercially for worship and group work without written permission from the publisher. If photocopies of small sections are made, please make full acknowledgement of the source, and report usage to the CLA or other copyright organisation.

The Iona Community has asserted its right in accordance with the Copyright, Designs and Patents Act, 1988, to be identified as the author of this work.

Overseas distribution
Australia: Willow Connection Pty Ltd, Unit 4A, 3–9 Kenneth Road, Manly Vale, NSW 2093
New Zealand: Pleroma, Higginson Street, Otane 4170, Central Hawkes Bay
Canada: Bayard Distribution, 10 Lower Spadina Ave., Suite 400, Toronto, Ontario M5V 2Z

Printed by Bell & Bain, Thornliebank, Glasgow

Contents

The silence of God: A reflection, meditation and prayer for Holocaust Memorial Day, *Isabel Smyth*   7

An interview with Mrs Grumpy, and other dialogues and monologues for worship, *Jan Sutch Pickard*   11

Women at the well: Remembering the Bible with women, *Janet Lees*   21

My gran's porch: Prayers by and for kids, *Ruth Burgess and Thom M Shuman*   43

Jesus is back!: Lent and Easter resources for remembering the Bible with children and young people, *Janet Lees*   73

Lead me into life with you: Short prayers for Lent and Holy Week, *Thom M Shuman*   93

To walk the way of the Cross: Prayers of intercession for Palm Sunday, *David Osborne*   101

Walking in the wider world: Readings, reflections and prayers for Holy Week, *Peter Millar*   105

Out of our brokenness: Stories for Easter, *Jan Sutch Pickard*   115

Love endures: A hymn for Easter Sunday, *Jan Sutch Pickard*   121

Lord of the upper room: A prayer for the first Sunday after Easter, *Roddy Cowie*   123

A litany of laughter: A meditation, *Joy Mead*   127

Ascension and Pentecost: All-age resources and ideas, *Janet Lees*   133

Let us live your love: Harvest prayers, *David Osborne*   139

The granaries of heaven: A Harvest prayer of thanksgiving
and concern, *Roddy Cowie*   143

Nature, life and being: A meditative look at climate change, the
sacredness of all life and human responsibility, *Joy Mead*   147

A blessing for a new car, *David Coleman*   153

Seven days: Stories & reflections for the World Week for Peace in Palestine
& Israel, *Jan Sutch Pickard & members of the Iona Community*   159

Racial justice: A reflection and a prayer, *Iain & Isabel Whyte*   179

Prayers for Remembrance Sunday, *Roddy Cowie*   185

The light which illumines the world: Readings, reflections and prayers for
the four weeks of Advent, *Peter Millar*   193

Voices of longing, glimpses of hope: A script for six voices for the
beginning of an Advent service, *Elaine Gisbourne*   205

The appointment: A reflection on the Incarnation, *Tom Gordon*   211

The Gospel according to sheep: An alternative look at Christmas,
Janet Lees   215

The council of the Magi: A dialogue, *Richard Skinner*   221

In shop doorways and on street corners: A reflection, meditation, and
ideas for taking action on homelessness, *Ewan Aitken*   227

About the authors   235

The silence of God
A reflection, meditation and prayer for Holocaust Memorial Day

Isabel Smyth

Reflection:

The silence of God can be frightening and deafening in its reverberations and perhaps that is the reason people don't like silence. This is particularly so in the face of great suffering and evil. We say in the Christian tradition that there is *'no greater love that anyone can have than to lay down one's life for one's friends'* (John 15:13). This is true, but I wonder if there is not an even greater love, and that is to watch other people be discriminated against, suffer and die, to have one's heart broken and be powerless to do anything about it – to live with unrequited love, misunderstandings in relationships, powerlessness to help or solve another's problem. This can be like a living death, protracted over time.

Shusaku Endo's book *Silence*, now made into a film by Martin Scorsese, deals with this very problem. Where is God amid the struggle with apostasy, with the temptation to deny one's truth and firmly held faith, not to save one's own skin, though torture would make that understandable, but to save others from terrible torture and execution? Where is God in all of this? Why does God not speak, not act? This is the dilemma of the central character in the film as he struggles with his faith and the consequences of his fidelity or his betrayal. Why does God not help him? How can he continue to live while others have died and sacrificed themselves for their faith? How can he bear the shame and guilt? What meaning is there in this life now?

The theme of Holocaust Memorial Day 2017 deals with this very issue. In the light of the Nazi Holocaust and the genocides in Armenia, Rwanda, Cambodia, Bosnia and Darfur (described as the first genocide of the 21st century), *'How can life go on?'*. Survivor of the Holocaust and author Elie Wiesel has said:

> *'For the survivor death is not the problem. Death was an everyday occurrence. We learned to live with death. The problem is to adjust to life, to living. You must teach us about living.'*[1]

The theme for Holocaust Memorial Day challenges us:

– *How are people to survive in the light of unimaginable suffering? ...*

– *How can life be rebuilt after such trauma? ...*

– *How does a person cope with living when so many others have died? ...*

– What sense can there be in all this? …

– How can we who are onlookers teach others about living? …

– How can we find meaning in their lives and our own? …

These questions do not just apply to survivors of genocides. I am sure we all experience a feeling of hopelessness as we view on our television screens the violence and atrocities perpetrated not just in the Middle East or parts of Africa and Asia but also on European soil. We ask: How can I live a comfortable life at home, speaking out about justice, doing my best to make the world a better place in my own small way – while all this suffering is happening all around, and I have personally experienced nothing of it? Where is God? Why is God silent? Is God's heart not breaking? Does God hear our cries? Does God shed tears over the pain and suffering, to say nothing of the evil of people, made in the image and likeness of God, whom God loves?

Our Christian faith tells us yes, God does, and the evidence for this is the Cross. Is the Cross not a sign for us that our God, however we understand God, feels deeply the pain and anguish of seeing people suffer? Does the Cross not show us that God fully enters into that suffering, that God is not far or distant but present in the very suffering itself? Christian belief is that to enter into this pain, to feel it deeply and embrace it, can lead to transformation and resurrection. The suffering and evil need not have the final word.

The systematic and mechanistic horrors of the Holocaust let loose a great evil in our world. They revealed the depravity that we all are capable of. Yet we know that we humans are also capable of great love and compassion. Believers of all faiths and none are called to confront this evil in ourselves and in our world, to acknowledge it and so weaken its power over us, to work for personal transformation and the spread of God's reign among us by lovingly:

- *recognising the interrelatedness of all people and refusing to divide the world into 'us' and 'them'*

- *accepting that both the perpetrators and the victims are our brothers and sisters and so feel the pain of the world and our implication in that pain*

- *keeping alive the memory of all those who have suffered and died for no other reason than their ethnic or religious identity*

- *rejoicing in and respecting diversity, recognising that difference of beliefs, cultures, traditions enriches our human family*

- *learning about the beliefs and traditions of those who are different from us, and challenging misconceptions and prejudices*

- *developing an open and generous theology that creates a place for people of all faiths and none in the heart of God*

- *looking out for, and supporting in a spirit of optimism, the signs of goodness and heroism in our human family, believing that goodness will triumph in spite of evidence to the contrary.*

Meditation and prayer:

- Imagine our beautiful blue planet …

- Hold it in your heart …

- Feel its pain and suffering …

- Feel, too, its goodness and energy: the energy of all those who work for its healing …

- Send out your own loving energy and healing as we pray together:

May the Lord bless you and keep you.
May the Lord let his face shine upon you and be gracious to you.
May the Lord uncover his face to you and bring you peace.

Source:

1. Quoted by the Holocaust Memorial Day Trust:
https://www.hmd.org.uk/news/we-launch-theme-hmd-2017-how-can-life-go/

An interview with Mrs Grumpy,
and other dialogues and monologues
for worship

Jan Sutch Pickard

An interview with Mrs Grumpy (Exodus 16)

The reporter introduces the interview, speaking directly to the congregation, and then turns to Mrs Grumpy, asking the questions one by one and leaving time for Mrs Grumpy to answer each of them. At the end, the reporter speaks directly to the listeners again.

Reporter: I'm standing in the wilderness, just over the Egyptian border. There are big crowds here, and earlier on they were holding a demonstration. I'm going to speak to a woman who seems to have been one of the ringleaders. Hello, Madam, I understand you are called Mrs Grumpy. And you *do* seem to be quite grumpy. Can you tell me what's the problem?

- So what did your leader Moses say to you? …

- What happened then? …

- What did you say when this stuff appeared out of nowhere? …

- And then what did Moses say? …

- So what did you do? …

- Was there anything he told you *not* to do? …

- And, I'm guessing, Mrs Grumpy, that you and your family thought you knew better! …

- So what happened? …

- Mrs Grumpy, if you had enough food every day, why did you try to get more than you needed? …

- Thank you, Mrs Grumpy, for answering my questions so frankly.

This is your reporter *(name)* returning you to the studio, after a very interesting interview, which has left me with even more questions – particularly about why these people grumbled so much, and seemed so ungrateful for what God was doing. Why was Mrs Grumpy so greedy? …

Another interview with Mrs Grumpy (Exodus 17)

The reporter introduces the interview, speaking directly to the congregation, and then turns to Mrs Grumpy, asking the questions one by one and leaving time for Mrs Grumpy to answer each of them. At the end, the reporter speaks directly to the listeners again.

Reporter: I'm standing in the wilderness. Since our last broadcast we've travelled some way from the Egyptian border, and have reached a place called Rephidim. There are big crowds here, and earlier on they were holding yet another demonstration. A woman here seems to be a spokesperson. Hello, Madam, I understand you are called Mrs Grumpy. And you *do* seem to be quite grumpy. Can you tell me what's the problem?

- So you were in dispute with your leader, Moses? …

- What did Moses say? …

- And the crowd's response? …

- What did Moses do then? …

- And then what did Moses say? …

- Were you getting ready to stone him? …

- I heard that he was waving a stick – was that to defend himself? …

- He did *what*? …

- What happened then? …

- Mrs Grumpy, did you and your companions trust Moses any more after this had happened? …

- And God? Did you trust God? …

- So what good came out of this incident? …

- Thank you, Mrs Grumpy, for answering my questions so frankly. This is your reporter *(name)* returning you to the studio, after a very interesting interview, which has left me with even more questions – particularly about why these people grumbled so much, challenged their leaders and seemed so ungrateful for what God was doing.

Good enough (Matthew 1:18–25)

Joseph: I've had enough! This would try the patience of a saint; and I don't think I'm a saint, just a man of principle. Just an ordinary mortal, minding my own business – Joiner and General Household Repairs – trying to do my best with the gifts God gives me: Behold the handyman of the Lord!

Folk appreciate good workmanship. On the whole they respect me: a solid member of the community. I never set out to be clever but want to do what's right.

And now this – what will folk say? Mary – my intended – she's going to have a baby. It's not mine. It can't be mine. What will folk say? Nazareth is a small town. Everyone knows everyone else's business. This isn't going to be good for trade – I'll be a laughing stock. I'll call the wedding off: quietly of course – that must be the right thing.

Angel: Joseph!

Joseph: That's me – Joinery and General Household Repairs, prompt service and cash terms. Who called?

Angel: I did.

Joseph: Who are you?

Angel: An angel of the Lord.

Joseph: I must be dreaming.

Angel: You are.

Joseph: I must be getting back to work.

Angel: Joseph, will you just listen? You're as thick as two short planks.

Joseph: It's likely in my line of work. Well, what do you want?

Angel: You are a descendant of David?

Joseph: Yes: you see, David begat Solomon, and Solomon begat Rehoboam, who begat Abijah, who begat Asa, who begat Jehoshaphat …

Angel: *(hastily)* Thank you. Do not be afraid to take Mary to be your wife.

Joseph: But …

Angel: For it is by the Holy Spirit she has conceived.

Joseph: Well, I never …

Angel: I know. It was an immaculate conception. She will give birth to a son. And you shall name him …

Joseph: Jehoshaphat?

Angel: No – Jesus.

Joseph: What kind of name is that?

Angel: Jesus – for he will save his people from their sins.

Joseph: What, all our family? All the folk in Nazareth? All God's people? All the folk in *(your town/city)*? One little baby?

Angel: Yes – and so it will come true, what the Lord said through the prophet: 'A virgin will become pregnant and give birth to a son, and he will be called Emmanuel.'

Joseph: But you told me to call him 'Jesus'. I can't understand all this. I'm not good with words. Though I am good with my hands – yes, proud to be a manual worker.

Angel: Emmanuel is a special name. It may not be a family name, but God has work for you to do – loving this baby and bringing him up in your family. Emmanuel means 'God with us'.

Joseph: What, with the workers? With the folk of Nazareth? With folk in *(your town/city)*? With ordinary folk like us? Well then, 'God with us' is good enough for me. Mary! Mary! We're going to have a baby!

Us and them (Mark 8:1–10)

What a mess – how did we get into this?
Us and them.
Crowds out there, perhaps 4,000 people –
men, women, children, sick, well, impaired,
confused, stroppy, deserving, undeserving,
not coping, undernourished, politically motivated, looking for an answer –
a chaos of human need.
They'd been following us for days, were far from home,
footsore, thirsty, hungry.
We could see how this was weighing on Jesus:
so much hurt, so much need; what was most urgent?
'They've nothing to eat,' he said.
'If I send them away hungry they'll faint on the way.'

For goodness' sake!
What do you want us to do?
We're overstretched. The money's run out.
And anyway, how can you buy food in the desert?
Do you want us to turn stones into bread?
These people should know that there's no such thing as a free lunch!

Then he looked at us and smiled.
Hadn't we been here before?
'How much bread do you have?'
'Ummm … seven loaves,' we said –
because we'd made provision for our own need –

bringing them out and handing them over.
Jesus told that huge crowd to sit down on the stony ground.
He gave thanks.
Then he broke the bread – our bread –
and we gave it out to the people – their bread.
And the fish – oh yes, we had fish, too:
we're fishermen you know, we can do that.
We had the resources; sharing them was another matter.
He took the fish – our catch – he blessed it.
He told us to hand it out.
It was their free lunch (at the point of need)
and it was our free-giving.
There was enough for everyone.
There were plenty of leftovers.
Jesus sent the people home.
Were they changed? Were we changed?
Are we still us and them?
Has anything changed?

Mother-in-law story (Luke 4:38–40)

Well, you've heard that preacher, Paul, talking about his calling,
about how much the good news of Jesus meant to him.
He never met Jesus, you know –
except when he fell off his horse on the Damascus road.
But I met Jesus, face to face. He came into my house.
And it was the last thing I wanted to happen.

I was poorly – had a fever, took to my bed.
It vexed me because there was so much to do.
The children – I love them of course – but they're always underfoot.
And that big lummox of a fisherman Simon
never thinks of giving my daughter a hand round the house –
I wouldn't have minded if he was away working,
if he was bringing back food to put on the table.
But for the last few weeks he'd been
following this teacher Jesus, hanging on his every word.
You can't live on words, you know. We all need bread in our bellies, too.

Well, I'd baked the bread already, because it was the Sabbath.
But that morning I couldn't get out of my bed.
That's not like me – as strong as a horse, usually.
I could see my daughter was worried.
But I was burning with fever, my head was spinning, and I drifted off.

Some time later I heard voices.
Simon was babbling with excitement,
telling her that Jesus was coming home for supper.
What a nightmare – the place was a mess, there was no food prepared.
Though it was dusk and the Sabbath was just coming to an end,
someone would have to get cracking.
I tried to struggle out of bed, and just collapsed.
I was scared. I've never felt that ill before.
Suddenly, making a meal didn't feel that important.
I thought I was dying.
My daughter and the children were wailing.

And then, suddenly, everything went quiet.
I opened my eyes.
This young man was standing in the room.
I could see Simon bobbing up and down behind him.
This must be Jesus. A strange man, and me in my bed!
But all my worries and agitation fell away.
The room felt very peaceful.
He looked at me, with tender concern.
He reached out his hand, and he took mine, gently raising me up.
I was no longer dizzy. My fever had gone.
I stood up.
He looked me in the eye and told me I was healed.

What a moment. I'll never forget it.
What did I do?
Well, I said Thank you!
(I'm well brought up, not like that oaf Simon … though mind you,
it was him who brought Jesus into the house,
so that I was healed – yes, maybe he's not so bad after all.)
What did I do? What do you think?
I went straight to the kitchen, with my daughter in tow,
and we made a meal fit for a king.
For Jesus and all the folk with him.
That was my way of celebrating
the health he'd given back to me –
giving him the best I could,
hospitality with all my heart.

Argument on the road (Luke 9:46–48)

We were walking with Jesus, and talking on the road.

Some of us started to argue about who was the greatest, the most important person among us.

James pointed out that he – his family – had the biggest boat. With bigger nets. So they could bring in the biggest catch. And they are a big family – big in the village. Big noises – sons of Thunder! All that has to count for something!

Peter – well, he's just a big man: big in every way, big-hearted – sometimes big-headed – and definitely the strongest of us all.

Andrew started in the fishing, and left his nets, but he's discovered a gift for networking. He keeps bringing people to Jesus – has got the ability to interest them in what Jesus is about. Having someone like this can make all the difference in the team. I think it's sometimes called Public Relations – powerful stuff.

Levi said smugly that you have to be well-educated to be a tax collector, and quick-witted, too. He'd ended up pretty well off – before he became a disciple – which meant that he could give dinner parties, where Jesus could meet all manner of folk.

Judas – he reminded us that he looks after our money. 'Money's power,' he said. Yes, where would you be without bankers?

John said quietly, don't forget the women – we need fed – we need practical as well as moral support. We're lucky to have these women friends of Jesus – they do a lot behind the scenes. And if you're looking for strength of character, Martha's a woman who has courage and speaks her mind; she's a person to be reckoned with.

Biggest, strongest, cleverest, richest, best connected, most powerful, indispensable – we were shouting the odds …

Women at the well
Remembering the Bible with women

Janet Lees

Introduction

This collection is based on the remembered Bible (RB)* and is for both remembering women in the Bible and remembering the Bible with women (and men). I have been using the remembered Bible as a survival strategy with individuals, groups and myself for over twenty years.

To remember Jesus is the very heart of remembering the gospel. We remember Jesus when we tell stories about him, when we share bread and wine in his name and when our actions are directed by what we remember of him. We do not have to be inside the church, as it currently defines itself, to do this. Jesus no longer belongs to a confined space. He is risen and our storytelling celebrates that. Working out who Jesus is for us is called 'Christology'. Theologian Rosemary Radford Ruether said that *'your Christology is a merger of your own concerns and your interpretation of the Bible'*. So when an angry female student told me *'finding out that Jesus got angry, too, helped me to see him as more human somehow'*, she was working out her Christology.

RB storytelling is a good way of exploring 'the who' of Jesus. Some stories will speak more at particular times and in different contexts than others, so go with the stories that resonate with you. It is often better to try to retell a story in your own words than just read it out. There are various ways of using these stories and prayers and some ideas for reflection or discussion are included.

* *For more on the remembered Bible (RB):*

Word of Mouth: Using the Remembered Bible for Building Community, Janet Lees, Wild Goose Publications

Tell Me the Stories of Jesus: A Companion to the Remembered Gospel, Janet Lees, Wild Goose Publications

Meanwhile at the inn: from barmaid to scholar

During Christmas 2016 I was standing listening to a conversation about how the men who visited the infant Jesus were models for the rest of us. From my remembered Bible, let me tell you the story of a local barmaid and her transformation to scholar: just one wise woman.

So Bethlehem was full. Didn't I just know it?! Every lousy last room full of travellers from heaven knows where, and me on my flea-bitten back in several of them. There were endless pots to wash and food and drink to serve, not all of it that wholesome. There at 'The Key of David' they'd got hold of an old ewe from a rustler and were trying to pass it off as lamb. Well, I knew how that felt.

I hadn't had much time to consider what was euphemistically called the 'strange goings on'. I had enough trouble of my own trying to keep wandering hands at bay, avoiding the master's eye and the back of the mistress's hand. More folk kept arriving – and every last space was filled. I heard they'd put a young pregnant lass in the stable. Well, in some ways there was less vermin in there than inside the house.

I spent several mornings heaving up in the gutter outside. What I'd thought was a bad brew of ale was looking increasingly less gastric and more drastic. I didn't really have time to listen to or think about vague stories from drunk locals about angels and peace on earth. And there was always more work to do and no one else to do it.

Things began to thin out a bit once people started to get registered. Once done they left for their homes again. The master agreed that the young mother (she had given birth out there after all) could move into one of the inside rooms, and I was kept busy enough running food and water and whatnot up and down the stairs. She was quiet most of the time, thoughtful maybe, tired of course, and trying to get the hang of managing an infant.

One day an odd bunch of foreigners turned up, a sort of camel train. Said they were looking for 'one born a king'. 'Look all you want,' the master laughed at them. 'The only baby here was born in the stable and is now upstairs.' They went to look, and decided to stay over. That pleased the master because it meant more money. I cleaned out some rooms as best I could and found something for them to eat. They were serious, reserved gents but told an odd story of ancient wisdom, stars and a long journey with many twists and turns. They'd even been to Herod's court, which made us all shudder. But they were polite and didn't take advantage, even though the mistress kept hinting at how there were extras available, if they were interested. They weren't, and went to bed early.

Next day, we were all woken by noise and confusion. News had it that troops had been sighted. The little family and the camel riders suddenly all wanted to move on. Something about bad dreams. Well, I knew how that felt. I'd not been sleeping for quite a few nights, wondering what to do about my own situation. I was bright enough to know that my news would not go down well in the household.

The camels were loaded up and a couple of donkeys too. Seemed the family and the foreigners had decided to travel together. It wasn't the right way back for any of them but it was a way out for now.

Turned out it was also a way out for me. The mother could not travel alone with all those men. Who would help her with the baby? I would. I rolled my few possessions into a bundle and seizing the bridle of the pack donkey set off without looking back.

We were an odd bunch, the little family, the three gents and me, now an ex-barmaid – but something bound us together.

As we left, chaos erupted in Bethlehem. Troops went from house to house killing male infants and even toddlers, and maiming any family members who got in the way. Mothers wailed – there was a crescendo of pain that could be heard beyond the walls as we set our sights on Egypt. Somehow in the confusion we made it, though those were anxious days.

We left the family on the border and turned to cross the desert again. What – you are surprised I stayed with the three gents and not with the family of three? Well, it was a difficult decision, but I'd learnt a lot on that journey. To go to a new place and start again, a new life with a new story and identity: that attracted me. From barmaid to scholar might have sounded unplanned, unlikely and not without dangers, but I'd come to enjoy their company, their storytelling and wisdom; and amongst them I'd found myself valued and listened to. My own voice had begun to emerge as my belly grew with the child I carried.

For reflection or discussion:

1. Can you remember a time when/a situation in which you felt your contribution was being overlooked?

2. Does the voice of the barmaid change the familiar story, or is it essentially the same?

Salome: the birthing

This story, also about the escape to Egypt, links to an Ethiopian tradition that says it was Salome who accompanied the holy family. In an illustration of this story I saw in an Ethiopian Bible in the British Library, Salome was described as 'Mary's midwife'. This monologue could be used when reflecting on welcoming marginalised people today, like asylum seekers and refugees.

I went with them. Of course I did. I went with them because Mary and the child were still vulnerable. But I went because I was vulnerable too. When the Roman army swooped down on Bethlehem to carry out Herod's orders it was the last place any woman would have chosen to be. If killing babies was not horrendous enough there was the aftermath – murder, maiming, rape. One generation of children wiped out and another seeded so that nine months later another legion was born. Yes, I could have stayed but what would that have achieved?

I went with them. They kindly took me along. I was one of the sand people. I'd grown up in a nomadic family in the harsh desert environment. My skin colour was testimony to my origins and the wandering life we had led. Each family had its midwife and my mother had passed on to me the skills and knowledge to be the next. I had other knowledge to share too: the routes and watering holes were etched in my memory – a map for survival.

I went with them. And together we made it to Egypt. We were refugees. We reminded the Egyptians of previous hostilities and so were always outsiders. As a midwife I had a way into the community and as a carpenter Joseph had his. Mary was a young mother, and even though the child thrived she had much to learn. There were other young mothers with many mouths to feed. We survived by sharing.

I went with them. Some others went further on. They paid for boats to take them across the sea to heaven knows where. We didn't choose that option as both Mary and Joseph were sure they would go back eventually. And in due course they declared themselves ready. The news had come of Herod's death, and it was time to return.

I went with them. In fact I kept step with them on and off for the next thirty years or so. That's how I came to be standing on a hill with Mary as her son's life ebbed away. I'd been there since the beginning, and on that day I held her again with his life flowing out of him and as her life seemed to be ebbing away as well. When they took his body down, Mary held him as she had held him when he was a baby. She wiped his face. After a while we wrapped him in cloth. Then we took him to the tomb.

I went with them. The women this time. We went back to the tomb on the morning after the Sabbath. Mary was fragile, light in our arms as we helped her along the path. The other Mary went running – and came back saying the tomb was empty. We were astonished, and even afraid. When we got there the stone was moved, the guards were gone. Instead, a great gaping hole, like a massive wound in the rock face, confirmed he was not there. From life to death and then … to where? We did not then know.

I went with them. Mary and the other Mary called Magdalene, about whom a thousand rumours abounded. They did not want to stay and neither did I.

We went on another journey, further than the first. We found a place which welcomed us enough. We offered our skills and knowledge – there are always more babies – and our friendship. We survived by sharing.

For reflection or discussion:

1. Can you think of someone who 'was there' for you during challenging times? Who was it and what happened?

2. During the course of her monologue, Salome repeatedly says 'I went with them'. How has your life developed? Is there someone you 'went with'? Or is there a different refrain that might accompany/describe your journey?

Like women

We sometimes find aspects of other women's stories that resonate with our own. Here are some short reflections on some stories of women, starting with Miriam from the Bible. Edith is nurse Edith Cavell. Constance is Constance Coltman, one of the first women to be ordained in Britain. Hope is a teenager from Yorkshire.

Like Miriam

Exiled,
outside the camp,
skin peeling,
sadness seeping through me:
you punish me
for what?
But unlike Miriam
I will not return
after seven days.

Like Edith

You stand still
as in that last moment,
keeping a vigil for us
on the edge of eternity.
Your words echo
across a century
and I wonder
how to leave behind
what festers in me.

Like Constance

The same call,
the same college,
the same choice,

the same struggle,
even one hundred years later.
I see the hope burning in you:
may it burn again in me.

Like you

'Hope is my middle name,'
you told me yesterday.
How thankful I am
for you and all you stand for.

For reflection or discussion:

1. Does Miriam's story resonate with you, and if so, how? If not, why?

2. Which woman here, if any, do you connect most with and why?

3. If in a group, ask each woman to write her name on a piece of paper. Give out the names so that everyone gets a different one than their own. As one woman to another, can you write a few words about the way your stories might be linked? Give the papers back to the women named on them.

The morning after

We had plenty of those! We'd often be awake long into the night, talking on and on, enjoying ourselves with a couple glasses of wine – too many blokes with time on their hands, free of the constraints and responsibilities of family, jobs and so on. So we'd boast and brag about stuff, like you do.

We'd get into some silly arguments. You know the sort of thing:

'Who is the greatest?'

His answers were always unexpected. Like the one about the little child.

'Whoever welcomes a child.' And, OK, who wouldn't. I mean kids – of course you'd do what you could to help them out, try to understand. But then: 'You need to be last, not first' was more uncomfortable.

He reminded us of what we stood for – for supporting the weakest, helping the poor: for putting other people first. Those were the greatest things we could ever do. Not boasting. That was a lot of hot air of a night out with the lads.

Late nights and early mornings were ours by choice. We'd chosen to come with him. But sometimes we lost our focus.

On the morning after it was sobering enough to remember to keep to his priorities.

For reflection or discussion:

1. *Can you recall the feeling of a morning after an important event or meaningful late-night conversation? If in a group, talk about this.*

2. *If there was something you could ask Jesus for, what would it be and why? If you like, write a prayer or say a silent prayer asking Jesus for this.*

3. *What do you think the women who followed Jesus were doing when the lads were talking? And what do you think* they *talked about?*

'Who am I?' (Mount of Transfiguration)

The pace of the journey had always been hard. The circumstances in which we travelled were never comfortable. There were constant demands on him from both outside and inside the group. He pushed on. That's when we found we had climbed to the top of another mountain. These places meant much to him: isolated, quiet, an awesome view. It was in places like this that he often chose to be alone.

We were all still getting our breath when he started: 'Who do people say I am?' he asked. Some thought it was a trick question and stated the obvious: 'You're Jesus, from Nazareth,' said one of us, laughing uncomfortably.

He went on, going round the group, getting more insistent: 'Who do people say I am?' He came to me. 'Why do you ask us?' I said. He licked his cracked, dried lips, and said in a barely audible voice: 'Sometimes … I don't know *who* I am any more.' …

We all looked at each other. No one knew how to break the silence. Eventually, one of us said: 'I heard someone say you're John the Baptist.' That triggered them all off. 'Well, that's rubbish – he's already dead.' 'Herod got him, so what do they mean?' Another said: 'Well, I've heard Elijah'; and another said, 'Yeah, and Jeremiah.' We were all talking at once, trying to help, but not really in tune with his state of mind or what he needed right then.

The babble eventually trailed off into silence again. He looked up at Peter and asked him, 'Who do you say I am?'

I wondered what Peter would say; we all did. Peter, not always good with words, chose a few and tried them. 'That's easy,' he said, looking him straight in the face. 'You're the one we've been waiting for: the Life-giver. God is in you and because of you we have seen God.'

This time no one broke the silence until he himself did. He weighed up what Peter had said, and then he said: 'Thanks, Peter, you're a rock to me. I will build on what you've said. It is the key to God's plan, and you will be the key-keeper. But let's keep it amongst ourselves for now, OK?'

And we did as he asked.

For reflection or discussion:

1. Who do you rely on to provide balance and stability in your life? Who helps you in the moments when you 'don't know who you are any more'?

2. How do you feel about Jesus, the Son of God, experiencing moments of doubt?

3. Get some paper or card and draw round a key and cut out the shape, making enough keys for the whole group. Invite each participant to write on their cut-out the name of a person who helps to provide support in their life. Collect the keys together and pray for these people using this prayer:

*Life-giver,
we are thankful for key-keepers,
whose support gives us balance,
who help us to feel safe and valued.*

The woman at the well

I went to the well today. It was hot and dusty as I picked my way through the goats and their kids gathered in the small spots of shade. It was the middle of the day: the time I used to come for water. The time when there was no one else there. That's why I'd chosen it then. I didn't want any questions, looks or insults.

I peered over the side of the well into the inky black depths, letting the cool moist air rise into my face. 'Our ancestor Jacob gave us this well – you don't claim to be greater than him, do you?' was the phrase that echoed in my brain. I spoke it aloud and it resounded against the stones: *'greater than him … greater, greater, greater …'*

Pulling my head up into the glare of the sun, I slid to the ground and crouched by the wall of the well. My eyes were dancing as they adjusted to the sunlight once again. Was I alone? Was I?

He'd told me everything there was to know about me: the whole sordid story. Well, it seemed sordid then. The men, relationships, partners, or whatever you want to call them. He was right: they weren't husbands. None of them had stayed. I didn't know where any of them were now. Once that had mattered. A lot.

'You would ask him for living water,' he'd said.

Oh, how I wanted that water! Water was always important in our village. Drought or near drought was our constant experience. The daily walk to the well was dreaded. The jars where heavy, the sun scorching, the well was deep. Young girls and old women struggled and would hope not to have to go more than once a day. As for those of us who were on the edges of the village, the ones with reputations or the subject of gossip, we avoided the others and made our solitary way in the high heat of the day, hoping to get it over with quickly and get back to obscurity.

But he stopped me and asked for water. Yes, I was astonished. After a moment I looked into his face. He wasn't mocking me.

We had a conversation, the longest I'd had in a long time, and him a stranger too. But then *not* a stranger: a strange stranger who knew all about me, even though we'd only just met. It felt good to talk, but also odd. The feeling returned today.

How could he know me so well? And that water: could I really have it?

I told the others about him, about the water. I thought they'd mock, insult me, ignore me. Instead they went to see for themselves.

I look back on that day as the moment that changed my life. I stopped skulking in the shadows. I went back to getting my water with the others, facing up to them, not running away. If someone made a comment, I'd challenge them. Not in a nasty way, but firmly. I had a right to the water, too, whatever they thought.

After a while my confidence grew; I'd contribute to the conversations. If a girl or old woman couldn't reach the water, I'd help her get it. If a woman wanted help or advice, I might offer some. Gradually, I began to feel more accepted.

When my partner left me again, I didn't feel the need to replace him as so many times before. I could lift my head up; I could get my own water; I could live as a member of the community.

Since then, I've got by. Some villagers accept me more than others. The old tales still go round but so do new ones – about the man at the well and what he said to me. Some of my neighbours were also changed by the encounter. It made a difference. In that way he was greater than Jacob. After all, Jacob just gave us a well to gossip at. Jesus gave us life-giving water.

Poem

When we talked this morning,
conversation welling up, stories overflowing,
bringing the past right up to the present,
I thought of the woman at the well.

You told me your mother had fostered others,
of the relationships, the damage and the healing;
how she'd challenged social services,
and kept on loving.
I thought of the woman at the well.

For reflection or discussion:

1. *Was there a situation in which you thought about the story of the woman at the well? What was the connection?*

2. *Can you think of a story that has been life-giving for you? If in a group, talk about this.*

3. *Pass a bowl of water around the group: Each woman dips her finger in the water and places a few drops in the upturned palm of the woman next to her, saying: 'Receive this gift of life-giving water.' After each woman has received the gift, finish together with this prayer:*

Life-giver,
well up in us,
flow through our relationships,
strip away the old,
shine up the new.

May we return to our wells
and drink deeply,
ready to meet the challenges of today.

Clean living

This one goes with the Last Supper.

'I remember he washed our feet,' I said.

'Why did he do that?' the child asked, stilling for a moment, as the water dripped from her body back into the bath.

I folded her up in the towel and lifted her out onto my lap.

'Well, someone had to do it. Everyone was dusty from the street, and remember this was the Passover meal. It was important that everyone was ready. Besides, he had his reasons: he always had his reasons.' I began to dry her and she snuggled into me.

'He wanted to do something that night that would help us to remember him; remember him through all that would happen later. This was just the first of those things. He wanted us to remember that there was nothing he would not do for us, and so, too, there should be nothing that we not do for each other.'

'So he wanted you to wash people too?' she asked from within the folds of the towel.

'Yes, of course: wash people like I'm washing you now; but also do other things to help people. Things people don't really look forward to or always volunteer to do for each other.'

'But you're always washing me,' she pointed out.

'I know, and I like doing that, but many people don't like to wash people or think it's for other people to do. He was showing us that he didn't think himself more important than anyone else. He would do anything for anyone, and we should try to do that too.'

'I like it when you wash me,' she confirmed.

'Not everyone likes being washed. They think it's just for children, or old or sick people. He was showing us that it was for everyone. He was also showing us what kind of king he is.'

'How do you mean?' she said from inside her cocoon.

'Well, kings don't usually wash people, do they?'

'No, I don't think they do,' she said, beginning to sound a bit sleepy.

'So first he came into Jerusalem on the donkey, and kings don't usually do that. Then he washed our feet, and kings don't usually do that. And you know what happened next?' I prompted her.

But she'd fallen asleep. I lifted her up gently. 'Time enough to remember that later,' I said softly. Now it was enough to remember the washing and his words about clean living and helping other people, another of his priceless gifts to us. I remember it every time I wash my child.

For reflection or discussion:

1. How do you feel about someone washing you and why?

2. For you, what were the hallmarks of Jesus' interaction with people?

3. How do you live out Jesus' instruction to wash each other's feet? … What else might you do?

Eat, drink and remember

This one goes with the Last Supper too.

I looked around to see who was going to go get the bowl and towel. It would be one of us women. It always was. I was ready to go myself, when I noticed that Jesus had already gone and got them and was ready to wash the first feet.

Then Simon, of course, said: 'You're not going to wash my filthy feet, are you? They've got a reputation, these feet. Dirtiest feet in Jerusalem.' And he held them up and someone went 'Phew!' Several held their noses and stepped back.

Jesus met them straight away. 'Well, Simon, it's your feet or nothing. Just for tonight, give me your feet and I'll have all of you. I think I can just about stand it.' He looked straight at Simon who, the wind taken out of his sails, dropped down on the bench and plonked both feet into the bowl with a heavy splash. 'Are you sure my feet are enough?'

'Yes, Simon, this is all it takes. Remember that,' and he patted Simon's feet dry before going on to the next person.

I started to set the tables: platters, cups and bowls. Gradually, as the feet were washed, folk came to the tables ready to share the food. Jostling to sit next to Jesus, to get a good view, or to avoid someone they disliked, the group assembled and the candles were lit. 'Blessed be you, Lord God, King of the universe.' And we joined in the familiar refrains.

Talking also took over. There were different views on the day's events and how they added up. The city was full of Romans, as well as pilgrims. The temple was full of scoundrels – and we Galileans were out of our depth really.

As I brought food in and out, clearing away things, I put a large bowl down near Jesus, and then heard him say, 'The one who dips his bread in the same bowl as me. That one betrays me.' Every hand froze in mid-air. No one wanted to be the one. But we'd done that so often: shared the same bowl of food. Every night on the road for the last few years. 'Get on and eat it while it's hot,' I chided, and went out for some more, coming back just in time to see Judas leaving. 'You off somewhere?' I asked. 'Just got to see someone,' he mumbled and I didn't see him again until later, much later.

But now the tone at the tables had changed. Jesus was passing round some bread. 'Look, the stuff of the earth. Have some, all of you. It's like my body, broken for you.' They chewed on it with puzzled expressions.

Then he took the last cup, the one we keep until the meal is over for the final blessing, and held it up, letting some of the wine run down his fingers. 'Here is a new blessing for a new cup. A cup of wine like blood, my blood: a cup for life not death; a cup of promise and hope.' He drank and so did everyone else. And then he got up and left the room.

As he passed me standing by the doorway, he said: 'Eat and drink yourself. You've had nothing yet.' And then turning to look back into the room from the passageway he added, 'Remember me.'

For reflection or discussion:

1. *Which parts of the story of the Last Supper resonate most with you and why?*

2. *Some people think it was an event just for men. What do you think and why?*

3. *Which stories do you think of when you're sharing food?*

Burning

After a lot of banging, they finally opened the door and let me in. I stumbled across the threshold and staggered into the room as the bolt of the door was quickly replaced behind me.

'What is it?!' several voices demanded at once.

'Where's Cleopas?' asked some others.

'Romans got him,' I said between gasps.

'What do you mean?' asked one, breaking the shocked silence.

'Romans detained him at a checkpoint on the way here.'

The men exchanged glances.

'So there are checkpoints then?' said one. I recognised Thomas' voice, belligerent and afraid at the same time.

'What happened?' It was Peter now.

Someone had put a cup of water in my hands. My breathing was gradually returning to normal. I began to tell them what had happened after we'd left Emmaus – so excited and full of hope.

It had been more or less trouble-free, until we got nearer the city. We'd seen others coming away from Jerusalem, hurrying, heads down, faces covered. They'd not spoken to us nor we to them. As we got to the city gate we saw the Romans. There were a lot of them and we wondered what to do. We'd waited for a bit, crouching in the shadows. Several other groups approached the gate. They were stopped by the troops there. Questions seemed to follow. Some were allowed through; others were held back.

'They were letting women through, but not men,' I said.

Was there another way to get in?, we wondered.

It was Cleopas who suggested that we should go back round to the Garden of Gethsemane and see if we could get in through that way. I wasn't sure it would help but that's what we did. We were on the way there, being careful we thought, when a group of Romans stopped us. They asked our names – where we were going, what we were doing. We replied as confidently as we could: on the way from Emmaus to Jerusalem, to visit our family.

'Do you know what's been happening in Jerusalem these last three days?' the commander asked us.

We looked at each other, then shook our heads.

'What things?' croaked Cleopas.

'The arrest, trial and death of Jesus of Nazareth. Some of you people thought he was God, eh? Well, his body is missing now and we're looking for it. Know anything about that, do you?'

We shook our heads again.

'They're just country bumpkins,' said one soldier. 'Leave them.'

'No, take him. Let her go,' said another.

'Go on then.' A soldier prodded me. And I ran all the way.

Mary, the mother, took the now empty cup out of my shaking hand and gave me a piece of bread and urged me to eat. 'You're in shock,' she said. 'Take your time. Tell us what else happened. What happened at Emmaus that caused you to take such a risk and come back tonight?'

I looked into her face. She'd been there at the end on the hill as we women had waited for him to die. The bread lodged in my throat. I swallowed several times.

'We've seen him,' I said. 'We've seen the Lord. He met us, and spoke to us, and then he ate with us. We came to tell you. To tell you what he said.'

'How do you know it was him?!' Thomas again.

'It was him,' I said simply. 'It was. It was like a fire burning inside us when he spoke to us. It was him.'

Thomas made a noise in his throat. It broke the silence that had greeted my words. 'I'll go and see if I can find out anything about Cleopas. Will anyone come with me?' A couple of others peeled themselves off from the group and the door was opened carefully. Their steps sounded down the alley and into the Jerusalem night.

For reflection or discussion:

1. *If you were to tell a story about the events of the first Easter which would you choose and why?*

2. *What do we learn about being a woman and following Jesus from these stories?*

A Matthias moment

I was once attending a meeting of local Christian leaders on the feast day of Saint Matthias. The meeting was going on a bit, and so I wrote this.

I knew Matthias. I lived with him in this small house for many years. Oh, I know it's not a glamorous part of the city, not fashionable or anything, but it's home. We both grew up round here and know the people. I've helped my neighbours: babies to elderly people. He helped in his own way: running repairs, lending tools and time. We were just an ordinary household, nothing special.

He knew Jesus, of course. They met years ago, before the wilderness adventure, before the encounter with John the Dipper. They'd meet up from time to time; see each other on the road or in a village somewhere. Jesus even came here once, but it wasn't a big public event: just a quiet meal, words to remember and a place to rest.

But Matthias wasn't one of the 12 who went with him from Galilee to those last days in Jerusalem. It wasn't because he didn't love Jesus, or because he wasn't moved by the things Jesus said. He was. It was *because* he was moved that he didn't follow them around. He thought a lot about what Jesus said and he said it changed his life. As a result, he ran his business differently and he treated other people fairly. He spoke up for people in the town square and he tried to offer support to all sorts of folk the rest of the community shunned. He said this was what Jesus wanted. But there was no need to keep trailing round from town to town. He'd go back from time to time to check out that he'd understood and was on the right track. Jesus always seemed pleased to see him.

Of course he was gutted not to be there at the end. He missed the Last Supper, but from what he heard it was just like the one he shared at our house a few months previously. He wasn't there at the trial or crucifixion – but then not many of the men were. He heard the Easter stories and said they made sense, confirmed what Jesus had said; and he was happy to affirm his faith in him even though he'd not seen Jesus again himself. He said many would share that experience.

So it was a surprise to me when he went to meet them one night – I mean the 11 who were left – and came back saying he'd been elected one of the 12! I didn't realise it meant so much to him. For a short time, until after that momentous day when they said the Holy Spirit came, he hung out with them and I saw little of him. But eventually he returned to our house and this little community. From time to time stories would trickle back to us of the others, taking journeys here and there, while he stayed here and got on with trying to live alongside the people he knew, passing on the stories, living the faith as he'd received it.

You want to know what happened? Well, look around you.

For reflection or discussion:

1. *If you were to choose a story to remember about Jesus, which one would it be and why?*

2. *What does being a disciple of Jesus mean to you?*

3. *How do you think telling stories contributes to us following Jesus together?*

4. *Which direction is Jesus asking you to take now?*

Final prayer

Calling One,
you keep right on
through the barriers erected to confine us,
beyond the mindsets that threaten to engulf us,
past the limits set to define us,
affirming and confirming even in our darkest times.

May the stories we create,
the crucible of ideas in which they float
and the well from which they spring
continually be a living force in us,
keeping us alive to your life amongst us
and the kin-dom you are making
from the fragments of our hope and love.

My gran's porch
Prayers by and for kids

Ruth Burgess and Thom M Shuman

Most of the kids' prayers here were written by 7-9-year-olds in the 1970s and '80s in a day school, and collected by editor/writer Ruth Burgess, who worked with the children. Some were used by the children at the beginning and end of the day. The Christmas and Easter words were sent round the school in an illustrated card. Other prayers here were written at different times and places. There are some poems and stories too. The prayers for kids were written by Thom Shuman, who is a pastor and writer in Ohio. Some of these pieces were originally published in: *Acorns and Archangels, Bare Feet and Buttercups, Candles & Conifers, Eggs and Ashes, Friends and Enemies, Hay & Stardust, Moments of Our Nights and Days* (Ruth Burgess, Wild Goose Publications). Whether you're a kid or a kid at heart, I hope you find these pieces helpful, comforting, moving, entertaining, fun …

– Neil Paynter, Wild Goose Publications

Family

Dear God,
please would you make my sister
not afraid of spiders?

Jean Marie, aged 7

Dear God
give some water to people,
and help my mam and dad and brothers and sisters
and me.

Gary

Thank you God
for my mam and dad
and thank you
for my nana and grandad
and uncle and aunties.

Tony

Dear God,
I hope you are looking after my family in heaven.
I would love to see my grandad and my nana again.

Tony, aged 8

Night prayers

Dear God,
please can you turn a nightmare
into a dream?

Dear God,
sometimes I am scared of the dark,
so look after me.

Dear God,
I wish I could have a big bed to myself.
If I did I would sleep in all day.

Dear God,
please protect me at night
because I am frightened.
Can you stop my horrible dream?
I shout out at night.

Dear God,
please let the night
be safe and nice.

Marie, Tony, Gemma, Jonathan, Candy, aged 7 and 8

Dear God
on the night
do not make me afraid.
I hate a creaking noise,
it scares me.

Paul

Keep me safe by day and night,
and outside every night
no strangers following me,
please God
Amen

Claire

Help

Dear God
can you stop all the wars?

Lee

Our Father
please don't get me into trouble fighting
and let me live all my life.
Please do it.
Amen

Lee

Dear Father God
help us not to be bad and wicked to other people.
Help us to share things and be happy
for Christ of the Lord.
Amen

Jade

Dear God,
please look after me
and make me do stuff right.

Gemma, aged 8

Dear Father Good,
please help me not to be cheeky
and be helpful to my teacher.
Amen

Ashton

Dear Lord
help us to be bright and cheerful and good.
Amen

Philip

Dear God,
I wish I had a car in the back garden but dumped.
Dear God,
I wish I could drive now.

Robert, aged 7

Dear God
forgive me for the bad things that I've done
and remember me when I was good like you.

Paul

Dear God,
I hope when I go to the doctor's tonight,
I hope he doesn't put a needle in it.

Marie, aged 7

Dear God,
you are the bestest friend I have got, then my mum.
Please help us.
You're my friend.

Michelle, aged 8

Thank You

Dear Lord,
thank you for all the music we can make.
Thank you for things we can do
like read and wright.

Martin, aged 8

Dear Lord
thank you for all the wonderful things in our world.
Help us to be bright and cheerful.

Christopher

I like God
'cause he gives us food
Amen

Dear God,
I wish I could see you today.
I bet you are nice.
I hope you are looking after Jesus.
Thank you.

Lee, aged 7

Dear God
thank you for animals
and people
and plants.

Lee

People

People rush
to get a bus
to go to work
every day,
to get the money
to buy the food
for the family.

John, aged 8

Posh people
cockney people
all kinds of funny people in the shops
and in the steeple
posh people
go to church every Sunday
cockney people get up late
and never go to church

Janice

School

Bullies

There they go strutting about,
nearly always with a pout!
They always shout: 'Get out my way.
You had better do as I say!'
If we do one thing wrong –
they'll give our heads one big dong!
I'm really scared of that dude –
one day maybe he'll strip people nude!
But I've just got to think about it:
why they're like that, just one bit.

Maybe they got bullied in their day.
Possibly that's what God will say.

Annie Sharples, aged 12

A prayer for a test

Dear God,
I have a test tomorrow:
please help me to do my best.
And help me to know
if I do poorly
that you'll still love me
just as I am.
Please help me to remember
that you are always there beside me,
every second of the day.
Thank you, Lord.
Amen

Annie Sharples, aged 12

New school

I'm in a new school today,
I'll never know what to say.
Everyone's here or there.
Sometimes people even swear!
Everybody has their mates,
I'm just sitting there by the gates.
I really hope I'll get a 'bud'.
Someone just really should
just happen to come my way –
and ask if I'll come and play!
So here I am on my tod.
But I have someone to talk to,
and that's God.

Annie Sharples, aged 12

Dear God
did you go to school?

Damen

Holidays

People go to work
to get some money
to go on holiday
to have fun
to go to the seaside
to get shells.

Paul, aged 8

Dear God,
thank you for all the holidays off school.

Christopher, aged 7

Lord Jesus, thank you for our holidays, for fun, to run.
Thank you for walks and talks.
Thank you for all the nice colours on holidays,
and all the people who don't have them, we pray for.
Thank you for our holidays, this year, and the next?
Amen

Annie Sharples, aged 8

Dear God,
thank you for holidays and fun, wildlife and nature,
and for walks and autumn colours.
Thank you, O Lord, for holidays.
Amen

Mary Sharples, aged 9

Christmas

On Christmas Day at half past three in the morning I woke up and I saw light coming out of my window – I thought it was light – but it wasn't light – it was just a lamppost making shadows – so I started opening my presents and when I was on the second before the last one my daddy came in and said, 'Put the presents down and try to get back to sleep.'

Graham, aged 8

Christmas is …

Christmas is making a mess.

Christmas is when Santa comes down the chimney.

Christmas is ripping my presents open.

Christmas is when the church bells ring.

Christmas is when it is Jesus' birthday.

Christmas is bursting balloons.

Christmas is when my dad goes drinking.

Christmas is when we light candles.

Christmas is when we get a new dog's bed for our Lucy.

Christmas is when we sing in the choir.

Christmas is when I am Joseph in a play.

Christmas is giving.

Christmas is when I say a prayer.

Christmas is when you can have a big dinner.

Christmas is celebrating Jesus.

Christmas is decorations on the tree.

Christmas is when we give our mums a present.

Christmas is when you hang your stockings up.

My gran's porch 53

Christmas is when I can choose what I have for breakfast.

Christmas is when you can play games in the house.

Christmas is a time for my belly.

Christmas is when you get Christmas cards for people.

Christmas is a time for making things.

Christmas is the giving day.

Christmas is when we sing carols.

Christmas is the time when Father Christmas comes and you get toys.

Christmas is when you have a cake.

Christmas is when we play with the snow.

Christmas is when you are very very excited.

Christmas is happy.

A class of 7-year-olds

Dear God
I hope on Christmas Day my family will be happy.
I can get some new roller boots
if you will tell Father Christmas I've been good.

Love Gemma, aged 7

My pop is lonely
and on Sunday
he comes to our house
and he has a dinner,
and on Christmas
he stays
and he goes in
a pub.

Gary

Holy Week/Easter

I don't understand adults

A boy in the crowd watches Jesus carry his cross.

I don't understand adults.
They make me angry sometimes.
Look at them now,
treating Jesus like a piece of dirt.
What has he done to be treated this way?
I met him once in our village.
His friends had been shouting at each other.
I'd watched them from the other side of the road.
Jesus called me over to him.
I was shy of strangers.
My mum had told me to be careful,
but I'd seen him before telling stories
and I'd listened to him.
He had some good ideas.
Jesus asked me what I enjoyed,
and I told him about the games I play with my friends.
He knew what I was talking about.
I told him about how I always got the blame when I row with my sister.
He knew about that too –
he'd had little sisters as well.
I like Jesus.
Grown-ups don't always listen to me
but I can talk to him,
and he listens and understands.
I feel sorry for him today.
I'm angry with the people who are hurting him.
And where are his friends?
Why aren't they sticking up for him?
Why have they all run away?

Ruth Burgess and Andrew Softley, aged 12

Why is he getting wrong?*

A child in the crowd watches Jesus carrying his cross through the streets of Jerusalem.

It's not fair!
Why is he getting wrong off the soldiers?
He's a good man.
Everyone knows him.
He helps people.
He makes them better.
He talks to people.
He tells stories – good stories.
Everybody listens to him.
Look at them!
Why are they hurting him?
Why won't they leave him alone?
He's not a bad man.
He's a kind man.
It's not fair.
Why is he getting wrong?

Ruth Burgess and Kirsty Langlands, aged 10

(*'Getting wrong' is a phrase used in the northeast of England and means 'getting into trouble' or 'getting blamed or punished'.)

Easter is …

Easter is when Jesus' friends are happy.

Easter is when the Easter bunny comes.

Easter is when my mum won't tell me where she's hidden the Easter eggs.

Easter is nice and good children.

Easter is decorating eggs.

Easter is when my sister eats my Easter eggs because I don't like chocolate.

Easter is when Jesus was brave.

Easter is finding eggs in the wash house.

Easter is when you get up early and eat all day.

Easter is when we go yummy for eggs.

Easter is getting fat.

Easter is when the stone moved.

Easter is starting a new life for baby chicks.

Easter is when you dance about.

Easter is when Jesus came back alive.

Easter is sharing eggs.

Easter is when we get lots of surprises.

A class of 7-year-olds

Seasons and the weather

Dear God,
what vitamin did you put in water
to make plants and flowers grow?

Peter, aged 8

Dear God,
can you stop rain
in Tyne and Wear?

Marie, aged 7

Dear God,
how does the rain come down?
Do you squeeze a cloud,
and is it like a dishcloth to you?

Joseph, aged 8

My gran's porch 57

Dear God,
I don't like it when it is a dull day.
It rains and the clouds are grey.
Please try to make our days sunny.

Andrew, aged 7

Prayers for kids, by Thom M Shuman

God

I hear about how
mean and angry
you are, but
if your lap is
soft as gram's,
if your breath
is as sweet
as dad's when
he reads to me,
if your arms
are as strong
as mum's when
she hugs me,
I think I could
like you.

When I grow up

God, do I really need
to leave my
imagination
in the closet,
my compassion
for my bullied friends
in the drawer,
shove under the bed

my joy at watching
clouds change shape
when I grow up? …

Getting lost

I think I
need a GPS
in my brain, or
at least a map
tattooed on my
hand, so
I won't keep
getting lost, and
wondering where I
am until I get
so scared I
can't think.

Be with me, God. Thanks.

Friends

Was it something
I said (or
forgot to)?
Did I laugh
at a joke and
they thought it
was because of them?
Did I do something
I shouldn't?
I don't know, but
suddenly my friend
won't speak to me
or notice me
and I can't figure
out why … can you, God?

Beatitudes for kids

Blessed are those who ask questions,
  for they are God's imagination.
Blessed are those who hug outsiders,
  for they are God's hands.
Blessed are those who comfort scared little kids,
  for their fears will disappear.
Blessed are those who stand up to bullies,
  for they are God's hope.
Blessed are those who eat lunch with the lonely,
  for they will be fed with grace.
Blessed are those who care for the homeless,
  for they are God's welcome.
Blessed are those called every name possible,
  for God knows your heart.
Blessed are the atheist and the believer,
   the Buddhist and the Hindu, the Jew and the Muslim,
   the wonderer and the wanderer,
    for you are God's children, all of you, each of you.

Parents fighting

Okay, God,
I put in
my earbuds so tight
so I won't
hear my mum
yelling about my
dad's boozing, and
him accusing her
of spending too
much money,
and I
wonder if I
will ever hear
them say
'I love you'
to one another
without it being
for show
in front of me.

Moving in with family

Now that mum
has lost her job,
she and dad say
we might have
to move in with
my gran and grandad,
but
they have trouble
keeping up with me, and

sometimes act
as if they wish
I wasn't there …

Suppose they say 'no'
because of me?

God, help us all get along.

Poor at sports

Were you picked last,
Jesus,
when the kids chose
teams for games?

Were you the one
sitting at the end
of the bench, always
overlooked by the coach?

Did you stand on the
pitch hoping (okay, praying!)
that the ball isn't kicked to you?
Did you know how much
it hurts to be so
poor and klutzy
at sports, huh?

I hope so, then
you know how I feel
every day.

Bullies

How do I tell
my dad
that the reason
my stomach always
hurts, or
mum that I don't
want to walk
to school any more,
is because I
am afraid of
the kids they think
are my friends (but who
pick on me
every day)?
Help me, God.
Be with me.

School worries

It's time to
go to school, God,
so please protect me
from bullies
who lurk in the hallways
or on the playgrounds.
From folk with weapons
who think the lives
of kids don't matter.
From friends
who make fun
of me behind my back.
From all the other
worries that wait for me
at a place where
I should feel safe.

Fear of the dark

Whenever anyone brings
it up, I join
in the laughter, the loud
cackles at the little
kids, but I
still leave the light
on in the closet.
I still worry about
the noises outside –
and the creaking
of the floor at 3am.
I sometimes look
under the bed
before I crawl in.

Answer me, O God,
when I call, and
store my fears
in your heart.

Keeping everybody happy

I tiptoe quietly
so as not
to wake dad up.
I make sure
my room is kept clean
so mum doesn't yell.
I steer clear
of my big brother
when his team
has lost a game,
or my sister
when her best friend
won't return her calls …

… It's hard to keep
everybody happy, God.

Body image

When I watch TV
or a movie,
and then look
in a mirror,
I am not like
any of those folk
with their perfect
hair, teeth,
bodies, smiles, so
help me not to be jealous
or down on myself,
but love myself as I am,
just as you do.

Getting along

Folk throughout the world
can't seem to
get along,
but in my class
there's a kid with a yarmulke,
a girl with a dot on her forehead,
a boy who wears a turban,
several Muslims,
and even an atheist or two
and we manage just fine,
so why in the world
can't the world?

Best friend

He was my best friend,
always greeting me with joy,
ready to listen to my problems
and to share in my wonder.
He was my pillow,

my comfort in storms,
my protector from danger.
He was the one who cleaned
my plate of vegetables,
and who finished my ice cream cone
before I was done.
My dog has died, God,
and I think the rain
is your tears joining mine.

Job loss

My mum has been looking
for work for months,
going out every day with
hope in her heart
and coming home sad.
My dad's hours have been
cut back by half,
and so we have to make sacrifices.
If everyone is so well off,
the word has not
reached my house.
Help us, God.

Food deserts

Kids in school
are always talking about
their overflowing fridges,
food that goes bad before they use it,
all the choices they have
at the local markets,
and every day, I go home
past boarded up shops
and weed-grown parking lots
wondering if today might be the one
where mum has found some

fresh fruit or veggies
without paying an arm and a leg
for such luxuries.

Prayer for a neighbour across the street

The fellow across the street
has been in the hospital
for a few weeks, having surgery,
and getting treatments.
I wonder if he will look
or act or be different.
I don't know.
So, help me to look
at him the same,
to treat him the same
way as always,
to just let him know
that we all care about him.

My gran's porch

It was on
my gran's porch
that I first learned
that you loved me.
It was in a bus
on the way to school
each day, when I discovered
what acceptance meant.

It was on the pitch
on all those rainy days
where I learned
what trust others means.

I've found a lot
of holy ground, God,

and not always where
I thought I might.

Loneliness

I've got
my mobile
my laptop
my own FB account.
I can text
whenever I want
and speed dial
the folk at school.
I can chat
with folk hours away
and have friends
I have never met.
Yet, I often think
loneliness
is my best mate.

We're all different

We're all different, I know:
some see letters backwards,
others struggle to figure out numbers.
Some need wheels on a chair
in order to get from place to place.
Some use their hands to speak,
while others read lips to hear.
A friend bursts out
with unexpected words,
while a neighbour gets
her food through a tube.
We're all different,
aren't we, God?
But just the same –
your beloved!

Racism

God, why is someone's skin colour
so important
that people have to call
others by bad names,
or scribble words
on their houses,
or phone them
in the middle of the night
to scare them,
or beat them up?

It's only skin colour,
not their heart,
their soul,
their life.

Fruits and vegetables

I like apples of every kind
but bananas creep me out.
I could eat green beans every day,
but Brussels sprouts – no thanks.
I get it that porridge is traditional –
but a full breakfast is so much fun.
I know that you created everything
to be good and healthy for us
(and mum is pretty insistent
that I clean my plate each meal),
but couldn't more of your creation
taste like chocolate?

Affirmation

Penguins waddling around
at the zoo.
The Northern Lights shimmering
in the sky.
The purple of the thistle
and the yellow crocuses.
The sun warming our days
and the moon watching over us at night.
Your imagination is awesome,
God of wonder.

People gathering to oppose
nuclear weapons
or to support the poor.
A rough sleeper
sharing half a sandwich
with her dog.
A doctor sitting by
an old man's bed
holding his hand.
You invite us to join you
in caring for those around us,
Jesus of the forgotten.

My breath on a bitter
winter morning.
The mist drifting
over the lake.
Winds stirring the leaves
awake from a springtime nap.
My mum giving me
butterfly kisses.
Your peace and hope
moves all around us,
Gentle Spirit.

Lord's Prayer

God, my friend:
your name is so special
yet I can still talk to you.
I long to live in your
space called grace.
May your dreams for the world
(and me) come true.
Give me the nourishment –
physical, emotional, spiritual –
I need each day.
Accept my apology
when I mess up,
and help me to listen
to those who tell me
they are sorry.
Hold my hand,
as I try to follow you.
Keep me from doing
what I know is wrong.
For you are
the heart,
the peace,
the hope
I need all my life.
Amen

Praying

When I am sad,
I can pray with tears.

When I am angry,
I can pray with clenched teeth.

When I am not sure,
I can pray with doubt.

When I don't know,
I can pray my questions.

When I am excited,
I can shout my prayers.

Every mood
every day
is different.
So my prayers
don't always need
to be the same.

Psalm 23

God is my comfort,
my companion in every moment.

When I toss and turn at night,
God rocks me to sleep.

When my fears chase me,
God holds my hand.

When I lose my way,
God brings me back.

As the shadows creep
closer and closer,
you are my light for this journey:

your compassion my walking stick;
your hope the shawl keeping me warm.

When I am surrounded by loneliness
you invite me home.

Setting a place for me
at the kitchen table,
you fill my plate with grace.

Turning down the duvet
in the guest room,
you tuck me into your love,
and I am at peace
always.

Jesus is back!
Lent and Easter resources for remembering the Bible with children and young people

Janet Lees

Introduction

'Jesus is back'

Alex, aged 12, walked into the Chaplaincy office on a Friday lunchtime at the end of the first week of the summer term. Easter was a fortnight behind us and I was trying to make a display of the work the Juniors had done leading up to Holy Week for the school Open Day, which was fast approaching. Alex began with his usual question: 'Have you got a job I can do?' Well, it was Friday, like I say, and there were heaps of things to do – choir practice was about to begin. My reply was 'Well, I'm trying to do this Easter display of the work the Juniors did in time for Open Day. If you can think of a title for it, print it off and put it on the board, that would be very helpful. I'll come back and look at it.' And then I went to the music department.

I was late back from choir of course: people stop and talk, it always happens. Alex had returned to his form for his afternoon session. I opened the door to the Chaplaincy. Alex had left the display board in such a position as I couldn't miss it when I stepped inside. The first thing I saw was his title. It read 'Jesus is back'.

It is because 'Jesus is back' that we have stories and resources to share in this collection.

The Remembered Bible method: beyond words

I've been using the remembered Bible method for over twenty years now. It all began after a period of study with Gerald West at the Institute for the Study of the Bible in Pietermaritzburg in 1994. Gerald's work is with texts: looking at interpretations that offer liberation to marginalised people. He calls this 'reading with' others. But as a speech therapist I knew lots of people who would struggle to be 'reading with', so I began to work on oral interpretations that did not rely on reading a written text. This has become *remembering the Bible* (or RB) – not rote learning but using remembered versions of the Bible narrative, which may be oral, visual or a combination, and developing interpretations through this approach that can be used by people of all ages and abilities. I've done three previous collections of this sort of thing, *Word of Mouth: Using the Remembered Bible for Building Com-*

munity; *Tell Me the Stories of Jesus: A Companion to the Remembered Gospel*; and *Coming in from the Cold: Advent & Christmas Resources for Remembering the Bible with Children and Young People* (Wild Goose Publications), which explain how to improvise or 'just go for it'.

Six years ago I took this approach with me to Silcoates School when I became the Chaplain and introduced it to the children and young people with the aim that they might reclaim the Bible as their own book. Some of the results are shared in this material for Lent and Easter. Much of it does not need to be used in a rigid and prescribed way. Try to get into the flow and see how it can release the remembered Bible in and with the people around you. Using RB is about merging ideas and hearing many voices.

Janet Lees

Resources and ideas for Lent

Introduction

At school Lent usually comes about the middle of the middle term, depending on the date of Easter. There are children and young people who grow up in pro-Lent households who want to learn the discipline of the 40 days. Some go for 'no chocolate' or 'no crisps', while others try putting money in a jar for charity or taking a prayer challenge. There are lots of ways to do Lent – and it's fine to find it bonkers too. The main focus is on Jesus and what he's doing, which is where the Remembered Bible (RB) comes in handy.

Pancakes

Traditionally in Britain, Lent begins with pancakes. As this is memorable and popular, we usually have a week for pancakes rather than one day. Check health and safety procedures in advance; if any of the potential consumers have food allergies, etc …

There are Lent cooking challenges, too, like using a small amount of money, while thinking about those in the world/community who don't have much money to spend on food and fuel; or try a Lent tradition from another culture.

Interpreting the Bible in Lent: Who is the devil? The Joker versus Batman

'Who is the devil these days?' asked a 17-year-old, as he examined the stones I'd placed on the communion table, to represent the stones Jesus is tempted to turn to bread. Good question: that is what interpreting the Bible is all about.

'I think the Devil would be like the Joker and Jesus like Batman,' answered one 18-year-old, and so we talked about acting out the encounter between Jesus and the Devil at the beginning of Lent. The two boys then performed the Devil and Jesus encounter … as the Joker vs Batman …

A conversation between Jesus and the Devil (Matthew 4:1–11)

This conversation between Jesus and the Devil was used by Seniors in sixth form.

Devil: Jesus, bet you're hungry. Jesus Christ, bet you're starving now. Forty days and forty nights – Jesus, that long. Bet you could turn those stones to bread – if you're hungry enough, bet you could, Jesus. Go on then. Jesus Christ, what's stopping you?

Jesus: Sure I'm hungry, Satan. Of course I could do that, you old devil. But isn't there more to life than food, than food got quickly – than fast food? And isn't there more to food than bread? Don't we need more than food to really live? Listen, Satan – listen to the Word of God.

Devil: Jesus, you're a dreamer. Jesus Christ, you're not real. Get up here and look at this. If you are God's Son, then jump why don't you? Jump from here, Jesus. There's angels who will catch you and be glad of it. You won't get hurt, Jesus Christ.

Jesus: So that's the next test, is it, Satan? Testing me again, are you? Think I'm losing it, do you? Think I'd try it even to please angels? Don't put God to the test, Satan. Listen to God's Word.

Devil: Jesus, you're not losing it. Jesus Christ, you've got everything to gain. Look at this mountain, bigger than ever. See all those kingdoms, Jesus. You can have it all, Jesus Christ. You can have the power over every one of them. Just kneel down and worship me, Jesus. Go on, just do it. What's stopping you now?

Jesus: Now it's you that's losing it, Satan. You know as well as I do that only God is to be worshipped and that we serve God alone. Go!

The desert again!

It's that time of year.
The pancakes have all been tossed.
From now on it's endless desert days and nights.
It's okay for you
and your macho desert friends,
practising your desert survival skills;
avoiding cooperating with the occupiers
by coexisting
with the revolutionaries
or the holy fools.
You manage to make heat and dust
look so easy,
surviving on what you can find,
but for us,
for whom barely a single snowdrop blooms,
this is not the place
we look forward to returning to
on an annual visit.
The desert may have
its moments of beauty:
still star-filled nights,
awesome vistas,
weather-etched outcrops
but as we enter the desert together again,
I wonder if we'll even find
the road to Jerusalem
on the other side.

Lent is here again (a hymn)

Tune: 'Linstead Market' (88 88 10 8)

Let us ashes for Lent deploy,
forty days we will now enjoy,
forty nights in which we will pray
seeking Jesus' way every day.

Chorus:
Lent is here again, we can start again.
Ashes mark us out: Christ's we are!

Tempted then to turn stones to bread
or let power go to his head,
in the desert for forty days
Jesus focused on God's right ways.

Chorus

Tempted now to think selfishly
or else ignore our neighbours, we
all get ready to give that up:
Pass the towel, the bread, the cup.

Chorus

Using the labyrinth in Lent: the way to Jerusalem

One of the most remembered kinds of silence we explored at school was when we used a labyrinth during Lent. We estimated that about two thirds of the children and young people in the school came to chapel to walk the labyrinth that week – we even had queues.

We collected lots of scarves and other lengths of coloured fabric to make the pattern of the labyrinth on the carpet. This is quite an easy way of doing it: you can make it bigger or smaller depending on the number of scarves and the space available; and it's easy to take up, put away and store, or take round to other groups.

The labyrinth is good for quiet reflection, for thinking about new directions, for praying and moving – for having a go.

We used the labyrinth as a space to reflect on 'the way to Jerusalem', the journey made by Jesus, and on our own journeys. A group would come into chapel, the labyrinth was explained, and one by one each student could choose to step out and make the journey. We also had free time to do this during lunch. Some chose to go round with a friend, and a team of girls went round it together when a match got rained off.

Labyrinth prayer

Patterns on the carpet:
light and shade,
coloured and plain.

Legs, feet
moving round and round,
in and out,
forward and back.

The sound of breathing
and of nothing:
we call it silence.

From Reception to Year 13
we created this
still space,
we relaxed
and enjoyed
the moment,
the movement,
the patterns,
the colours,
the air …
the stillness.

Lent prayer for refuelling (Isaiah 40:28–31)

God, I welcome your promise to refuel me.
As the passionate journey once again
takes the long and winding road
from here to Jerusalem,
I delight in meeting so many others,
as together we tread out a rich pattern
of following ways,
making the well-worn path
flower with new possibilities.
May we soar, glide and spin with all creation
as we join your effortless dance.

Lent is bonkers

Lent is bonkers:
you and me, God,
belting round the universe
sometimes this way
sometimes that.
There's those who say
'Be quiet.'
And I say 'Naff off.'
There are those that say
'Do it this way.'
And I say 'Not on your life.'
Folding paper,
painting faces,
holding string,
sticking notes on everything,
I cartwheel across
from one planet to another.
But there's a day coming:
you and me, God,
we know this day,
when everything hangs
in the balance

and the Lifegiver
gives it all up
that we may live on.
I've got it in my sights now:
my heart is racing,
I can't stop it.
Lent is bonkers:
so much for forty days and nights.
When only one day counts
this is the One we can count on.

Resources and ideas for Easter

Introduction

Easter is a key festival of the Christian Year, but depending on when it falls in the calendar it may or may not make it into the school year. Sometimes we are at school during Holy Week and sometimes we are not. Whatever the days or dates in the official calendar we sometimes have to alter things a bit to enable us to have the celebrations at school. So we've had Palm Friday on the Friday before Palm Sunday or even Palm Monday on the Monday afterwards. We've also had Maundy Wednesday for remembering the Last Supper or even a whole week of doing that in order to fit everyone in. On the whole, when using RB the ethos is it's better to have Palm Friday than have Palm nothing at all and miss it.

One cross, different voices (a dialogue for two voices)

He said we were going to Jerusalem – that's always exciting! I always look forward to that.

He said we were going to Jerusalem – that's always scary. I always dread that.

He said he'd be put to death, but I thought it unlikely. God would have other plans I was sure.

He said he'd be put to death, and I could well believe it. God's plans were a mystery to me.

He said he'd be raised to life, so I thought it would be all right after all. Nothing to worry about.

He said he'd be raised to life, and I thought maybe but maybe not. It was a worrying idea.

He said if we want to follow him, we must carry our cross. Not so long ago he said it was about fishing for people, sharing bread, offering life. I liked the sound of those. I'm not so sure about carrying a cross.

He said if we want to follow him, we must carry our cross. I remembered him asking me to follow him. It hadn't been easy. It sounded as if it was going to get even more difficult.

He said if we want to save our life, we'll lose it, and if we lose it, we shall find it. It's stuff like this that confuses me. But I do want to see God's Kingdom come.

Me too, but do we have to die first, and what does it mean? …

April Fool's Day

Palm Sunday may fall on April 1st, which in Britain is April Fool's Day. Even if it doesn't, it could be argued that riding a donkey into Jerusalem in front of the Roman army of occupation and the religious authorities of the day was a pretty foolish thing to do …

It was a foolish thing to do that day:
riding into town on a donkey
with people shouting and waving branches.
Who could take kingship seriously after that?
But two thousand years later we still remember it,
as we wait for the return of the green blade
and shout our own greeting.

Holy rider,
make us foolish enough
to follow in your footsteps.

The same coin

At school, Holy Week too will fall on different dates. Whatever dates they happen to be, the homophone week/weak makes a good contrast for this week of weeks.

At the beginning of Holy Week
it is as well to remember:
that strength and weakness
are but two sides of the same coin.

This coin has the face of Jesus
as both heads and tails:
strong enough to turn a table,
weak enough to spot a sparrow,
life flipping from one to the other.

As we approach Holy Week,
it is as well to remember
that staying strong requires
one to be wholly weak,
mindful of what it is to be fully human.

Holy Week diary

You could keep a Holy Week diary using the Remembered Bible. Link your RB to your daily experience in Holy Week.

Make each entry short and direct. Limit yourself to a few lines or a limited number of characters, a haiku or a number of kennings.

Here are some examples from Holy Week 2014. You could use these with some prayer stations or as short meditations in a Holy Week service. Best of all – make space for people to write their own pieces and share them.

Holy Monday

Across the blue sky
four swans scored a line
between heaven and earth:

their wing beats
challenging the laws of physics.

Holy Tuesday

How noisy the city can be
and how colourful.
All human life is here:
a young man tells us his story
unasked.

Holy Wednesday

It's a challenge
to be a fig-tree-curser
when your lips are sore
from sweet-fig-eating.

Maundy Thursday

We have each been
both betrayer
and betrayed:
like a dragon
biting its own tail
in a twisting Celtic design.

Good Friday

I walked in the woods
and heard the birds singing.
Was it for death or resurrection?
The tortured limbs littered the ground.

Holy Saturday

We leave you to rise,
Bread Man,

not in a warm place,
but in a cold tomb.

Easter Day

In God's eye,
pain when you were on the tree dying.
In God's eye,
grief when you were in the tomb lying.
In God's eye,
joy when you were in the garden living.

The Last Supper

Although we celebrate the Last Supper in our churches in our formal communion service, there are many other ways of remembering the Last Supper, with people of all ages, in and out of church. Here are some ideas:

For everyone

Set a large dinner table, as if for the Last Supper. Ask people to help you get it ready. What will you place on the table and why? How will you sit together and why? The Bible gives us some guidance about the context of the Last Supper but doesn't answer all the questions that will come up.

Use your common sense and what works in your space. If the table is not big enough for everyone to sit round maybe some can stand up; or take it in turns to have small groups at the table. Set the table up in a place where it can remain for a few days, or even a week, and then people can interact with what's on the table, etc as they have time. You may want to leave a prayer or two for people to pray and reflect on:

Prayer

Christ of the Last Supper,
despite our everyday betrayals,
you continue to feed us with your body and blood.
Hallow these preparations so that,
whenever we eat and drink,

whether in city or village,
as you were present in the Upper Room,
you will be present with us.

Blessing

May the Life-giving Spirit give us the grace
to examine ourselves honestly,
to share generously
and to wait eagerly for new life.

For young people and children:

If your young people are studying this part of the gospel in the curriculum, provide a 'revision session' for them going over the events recorded in the written Bible. We've used chapter 14 of Mark's Gospel for this.

Acting out the Last Supper is fairly simple (look at a Children's Bible for ideas). Lay out the table, then invite the children to sit or stand round it. One can be Jesus and the disciples can also be named. Try to get a wide range of children taking the roles. Depending on the age group you will probably find some want to taste the bread and 'wine' (use juice obviously). You will also find they have some questions.

Children could decorate a paper plate with things they remember about the Last Supper, with the words of Jesus or with pictures of the items on the table (have plenty of paper plates, pens and markers handy for this).

Word games

Word games can also be popular. Look at this pattern of words about the Last Supper:

Hand shakes, bread breaks.
Dark cup lifted up.
Poured out – heaven's shout!

In pairs or small groups, see if you can add or make up lines or couplets like this. Other words can be shared around the table, for example ideas about 'broken and whole', 'full and empty' …

*Take the broken bread
and celebrate the broken things
and the whole things.
Take the full cup
and celebrate the empty things and the full things.
For broken or whole, empty or full,
we celebrate our participation in the body of Christ.*

The table is also a good place for sharing silence.

Paintings of the Last Supper

There are many famous paintings of the Last Supper. One of the most famous – some say *the* most famous – is by Leonardo da Vinci. At the time it was painted the bread was thought so realistic it seemed to be real bread. The scene was modelled around the refectory table of a monastery, so it fitted the context of its time. Various other artists have created their own version of the Last Supper based on his image and layout. You will find versions showing women at the Last Supper, superheroes and even Daleks! There is also a Lego version. Search on the Internet for different versions of the Last Supper and talk about them.

You could draw/paint/make our own version of the Last Supper, or you could all pose around a table for a photographic version. What kind of table represents your community? What sort of bread and other things will you use? Have these on display in your school, community centre or church for everyone to talk about and enjoy.

Furniture

Bob Law (1934-2004), an artist, said this about the Last Supper: *'I'd made a few chairs and I was looking through some books one day and I saw Leonardo da Vinci's* Last Supper. *I thought, that's a good subject – everyone tries it so I think I'll have a go at it. I made it without the figures so that the broken chair is Judas' chair and the centre chair with the cross is Christ's chair – and then the other common disciples' chairs – and I made it in a most simple way, worked out all the proportions of the spaces between the legs and the backs, in wood, and then I had it cast in bronze'* (from www.artcornwall.org).

Bob's idea can be a talking point about the Last Supper, and particularly about the figure of Judas and the relationship between him and Jesus. Provide some chairs and see how the group arranges them.

Stuck in traffic

Traditionally Elijah has a seat at the Passover table, which remains empty awaiting his return.

Perhaps Elijah is stuck in traffic
and that's why he's missed
the bitter herbs and salt
and the rest of the Passover paraphernalia.
In his absence, we remember again
the journey from sea to cross.
If we forget a few plagues
we've added potatoes,
symbols of more recent journeys.
Singing Shalom, it is our Passover:
to remember one with us still,
even though other chairs are empty.

Why Good Friday?

The inevitable question is 'Why is it called Good Friday?' Why indeed?

'Why Good?',
you asked and I agree:
why Good,
what Good,
where God?

I say Bun Friday,
hot and crossed,
these traditions
I like the most.

I say Fun Friday –
school is out:

a real cool day
without a doubt.

I say Quiet Friday.
Solemn stuff,
time to think.
But can we laugh?

I say God Friday,
like every day.
Was God there?
What do you say?

I say Good Friday,
and wonder still
what was good
about that hill.

Good Friday prayer

Christ of the Easter vigil,
as you hung on for us,
help us to hang on
to and for each other.
Remind us that we all still count,
in that endless crowd of witnesses.
Confirm us as cross people
as we take the steps that lead us
from death to life.

Poem for Holy Saturday: Among the dead

Whisper softly,
speak in hushed voices
but do not disturb the dying.
Be respectful,
keep your eyes lowered,
as it dies little by little.

But you,
you who have already been in the tomb
three or four days,
who have smelt your own stench
and then emerged
at the call of the Lifegiver:
you are not afraid.

For you,
you who make up words,
who use your own given name
and dance on graves
flinging bandages about
celebrating release:
you are not afraid.
You already know
that no body is here.
There's no point in seeking the living
among the dead.

On not winning the egg

A short reflection from the last few minutes of spring term one year. There had been a raffle of a giant chocolate Easter egg for the local hospice.

I didn't win the egg.
But maybe that was just as well.
Two and a half kilograms of chocolate may sound great
but it's not recommended for your five a day.

And besides,
when it comes to meltdown Friday –
that day of all days
when we see what being human costs
face to face;
when we see the inhumanity exposed
in all its cruelty;
when we see the raw pain

and experience the long vigil –
can a chocolate egg really cut it?

Jesus is back!

Not only on the first day of the week but every day
JESUS IS BACK!

Not just in a garden but everywhere
JESUS IS BACK!

From sunrise to sunset
JESUS IS BACK!

For those who recognise him and those who don't
JESUS IS BACK!

So, leave the tomb, it is empty; tell everyone
JESUS IS BACK!

Lead me into life with you
Short prayers for Lent and Holy Week

Thom M Shuman

Ash Wednesday

Jonah 3:6

Yesterday,
fresh-faced and foolish,
I chased after all
the wonders of the world;
now,
ashen-smudged,
lead me into
life with you.

First Sunday in Lent

1 Corinthians 1:25

When we think
we will learn
all we need
at the feet of
great thinkers, sit
us in a room of
eight-year-old kids as
they tell those
silly stories that
crack you up.

Second Sunday in Lent

Jeremiah 1:9

When we are stunned
into silence by the
cruelty,
selfishness,
anger around us,

fill us with your words of
grace,
hope,
peace, so
we may offer them
freely, joyously, generously.

Third Sunday of Lent

1 Corinthians 6:12

When my desires
want to run
this show called
life,
let me simply
step aside so
you can
show me the
path.

Fourth Sunday in Lent

Mark 8:15

May the yeast
of your hope
prove us so
we can rise
to bring hope to
all those around us
who hunger
for it in every moment.

Fifth Sunday in Lent

1 Corinthians 9:19

Remind us
that when we serve
others, we
do not lose
our freedom,
but use it
to bring others
out of the prisons
of injustice and despair.

Passion/Palm Sunday

Matthew 21:14

Children hopping on one foot,
then the other;
some are
the forgotten hopping
from one moment to the next;
palm-wavers hinting
from one cheer to the next;

all of us having room
in our pockets
for the nails
freely offered to us.

Monday of Holy Week

Philippians 3:8

When we are willing
to give up all
that we value the most,
we find room
in ourselves
so we might
be filled with
grace,
hope,
peace,
you.

Tuesday of Holy Week

John 12:24

May
the tiny seed
of faith
you planted in us
on the first step,
now begin to bear
its bittersweet fruit
as your hour comes
closer.

Wednesday of Holy Week

John 12:35

When we find
ourselves in doubt's
shadows,
come,
to lead us
with that light
which our fears
cannot
quench.

Maundy Thursday

John 13:5

Slowly dipping
your hands in God's
tears which have pooled
in the hollow of your grace,
you kneel
and bathe us
in that love
death can never wipe away.

Good Friday

John 19:30

There,
as your heart empties,
as your voice falls into silence,
as your soul breaks into
a thousand peaces,
we are made whole.

Holy Saturday

Matthew 27:60

As chaos broods over
our shattered hearts,
God sits down
at a piano, sounding
out a tune never heard before,
and Spirit writes lyrics
no one will comprehend.

Easter Day

Luke 24:31

On this morning

let us see you
in every stranger;

let us hear you
in the whispered
hopes of hungry children;

let us welcome you
into our empty hearts.

To walk the way of the Cross
Prayers of intercession
for Palm Sunday

David Osborne

God, we think today of Jesus riding into Jerusalem on a donkey
like a poor labourer …

And so we pray for those who struggle to get by
because they are badly paid, or unemployed,
because of illness or disability,
because of prejudice or abuse,
or because they have had to leave their homes
to seek safety elsewhere.

We pray that those who suffer may know your justice,
that those of us who have the resources to help
may have the courage to do so,
and that those who make decisions
concerning the welfare of their countries or communities
may recognise their responsibilities towards all people.

God in your mercy …
Hear our prayer.

We think of Jesus fulfilling a prophecy of one who brings peace …

And so we pray for those caught up in war or civil violence
in Syria, Iraq, Turkey, Ukraine, Yemen, Palestine, Israel …

We pray for peace in your world,
that those who have it in their power to call a halt to violence may do so
and that those in positions of influence
may have the wisdom to see your way forward.

God in your mercy …
Hear our prayer.

We think of the crowds shouting and cheering,
acclaiming their Messiah with palm branches …

And so we pray for all who are carried along by crowds,
pushed by those who shout and shove around them,
or by social media, newspapers or television.

We pray for freedom and for integrity,
that in our debates about welfare, taxation or world affairs
there may be honesty and a willingness to listen,
and that in our social life
we may look for what really matters for our wellbeing,
for the good of our neighbours, wherever they are,
and the healing of your world.

God in your mercy …
Hear our prayer.

We think of the rulers in Jerusalem,
afraid they might lose their power …

And so we pray for all those who today have great power
as members of governments,
or because of their wealth,
or their ability to sway others by what they do or say.
We pray that they may use their influence for the good of all,
and that those who have little power may discover
the resources that are within and among them,
and that we may all have the courage
to use the gifts and opportunities you give us
in the ways that you intend.

God in your mercy …
Hear our prayer.

We think of the disciples walking with Jesus amidst the shouts of praise,
then leaving him when he was arrested …

And so we pray for ourselves –
with our struggles, our pain, our griefs, our gifts and our joys –
that we may know the comfort of your continual presence with us
and that, despite our fears,
whether things are hard or comfortable,
we may continue to walk the way of the Cross.

God in your mercy …
**Hear our prayer,
and let us know and live your love.**

Walking in the wider world
Readings, reflections and prayers for Holy Week

Peter Millar

Palm Sunday

The road to Jerusalem

Zechariah 9:9–10,16; Mark 11:1–11

At the beginning of our journey through Holy Week, we remember the journeys Jesus made to Jerusalem: brought as an innocent child in the arms of his parents; brought as a young boy, growing fast and full of questions and curiosity; and coming, again and again, as a grown man to the great festivals in the courtyards of the Temple; facing, with coolness and courage, the growing dangers, spoken and unspoken, the threats to his freedom and life. As he enters the city on this day, the crowds are cheering: 'Hosanna!' They see in Jesus the fulfilment of their dreams of freedom from occupation and persecution. Soon it will be different words they shout.

Prayer:

Lord,
thank you for your loyalty and patience towards us
who have so little understanding of what might lie ahead.
Thank you for your love which never ceases,
your forgiveness which never runs out
and your light that shines on in the darkness
and shows us the footsteps to follow
and the road to take.

Monday

God's tenderness

John 12:1–11

This well-known reading about Jesus being anointed in the home of Lazarus in Bethany is today being read in every land and in hundreds of languages. Through these verses we are linked to millions. Mary, the sister of Lazarus and Martha, took half a litre of expensive perfume made of pure nard and poured it on Jesus' feet in an act of total tenderness. Let us be challenged by such an act as we pray today for our sisters and brothers whose daily living is not marked by such gentle acts of compassion but rather by violence and disconnection.

Prayer:

Lord of this and every Holy Week,
grant me the gift of a tender heart.
It is easy to believe that we are all out for ourselves
and what we can gain,
but you show us another way:
the way that leads to true life.
The way of tenderly reaching out to others,
especially the strangers in our midst.

Tuesday

Letting go

John 12:20–36

Years ago in my parish in the East End of Glasgow we had a poster which said 'Let Go: Let God.' Simple words – but profound. And on this day in Holy Week we are called to immerse our daily living not just in our own endless preoccupations (which is easy to do) but in the heart of God. Ancient words put it this way: *'to die to self in order to gain Christ'*. This is not a journey we can do on our own: we need each other to discover the depths of our Christian faith, for the idea of 'dying to self' runs totally counter to our present wisdom.

Prayer:

Liberating Lord, free me –
at least sometimes during the day –
from being concerned only with myself!
Take away my inner blindness,
and help me to see that you are always calling me
closer to the One who created me
and to a new way of seeing your wonderful world
in all of its beauty and amazing diversity.

Wednesday

Jesus predicts his betrayal

John 13:21–32

This betrayal of Jesus was to come not from an outsider but from one within his close circle of companions. Jesus knew that very shortly Judas Iscariot would do him down. We may ask – how can a friend do that at such a time? The truth is we know that even close friends can and do betray us. And we ourselves can betray others, even if sometimes inadvertently. Let us today bring before God the ones we have betrayed and hold them before the Lord who heals and lovingly forgives.

Prayer:

Dear Lord,
you know my heart and my intentions.
And sometimes I act wrongly.
Be near today to those
I have betrayed or let down.
You know them and I know them.
Help me to see that we all stand in the need of grace.
Help me not to run away from my own failures
and to accept deep down
that I too need your healing touch today.

Thursday

The humble heart

John 13:1–17, 31–35

Here we read of Jesus, in humility, washing the feet of his disciples. It was a sign to his followers of a particular inner quality that was required of them if they were later to carry with integrity the Good News of the Gospel to others. When we think today of the way the nations are relating to each other we do not think of humility. Yet there is this 'other way' in human relationships and Jesus illustrates that for us and for all time. Humility is not lack of conviction. It is that dimension of the heart which allows us to accept and understand something of the other person without always imposing our own agenda.

Prayer:

God of every race and tongue,
may the peoples of our world learn again
to be humble enough to listen to one another
instead of rushing to easy judgements.
To be humble enough to admit to error.
To have the gift of humility
which enables the other to flourish as well as ourselves.

Friday

One Cross and many crosses

John 19:17–30

For 2000 years believers have come to the foot of Christ's Cross. The place of suffering and death: of loss, of violence, of ending. On this Good Friday we stand both before that cross and alongside our sisters and brothers who today carry their own crosses in many parts of the world. Their pain is no less than the pain of Jesus on the first Good Friday. We weep for Jesus and we weep for them. In the relative comfort and security of our lives we are faced with a basic truth: human suffering is endemic in our times. And at its heart is a suffering God.

Prayer:

Lord, as I think of your Cross,
give me the courage and grace
to be able to visualise those who carry a cross today.
Let me be near those who are tortured and abused,
those who are abandoned,
those who walk alone,
those who are being robbed of their dignity,
those who only know war,
and those who are being killed
because they believe in you.

Saturday

At the grave

John 19:38–42

Joseph of Arimathea, a secret follower, had asked Pilate if he could take the body of Jesus, and with Nicodemus he lovingly laid Jesus to rest in a new tomb close to where he had been crucified. We all know what it is to stand at a graveside. And weep. Jesus had passed on and only the silent body remained. Sorrow engulfed his friends and none of them knew what lay ahead. Every one of us has experienced this uncertainty and grief. Today we pause and allow our tears to flow – maybe unseen by others or more apparent. The tears of life: the tears of death.

Prayer:

God of both life and death,
thank you that we can experience sorrow in our lives
for without that knowledge were are impoverished in our souls.
Thank you for the times of our tears,
both inward and outward.
Thank you also that we understand the grief of others,
even those far away.

Sunday

The dawning of hope

John 20:1–19

In one of the great Scottish paraphrases – written generations ago – and sung in many churches on Easter morning, we have these life-affirming words. Let us take them to our hearts. May they grip our souls and our spirits on this special day: *'Nor death nor life, nor earth nor hell, nor times destroying sway, can e'er efface us from his heart, or make his love decay. Each future period that will bless, as it has blessed the past; he loved us from the first of time, he loves us to the last.'*

Prayer:

In the mystery of faith,
touch our life with the truth of the first Easter.
Help us to know we are never alone.
Help us to know goodness is forever greater than evil:
that light overcomes darkness.
Help us to know that your Spirit is deep with us.
Help us to know that this is the day you have made
and that, with all your people,
we can truly rejoice in it.

Easter Monday

Moving on

John 21:1–19

Here we read of how Jesus appeared after the Resurrection to seven of his disciples. Initially they did not recognise him, but then they became aware that the one who was with them by the lakeside was Jesus. They knew that they were not abandoned but held firmly in the wider possibilities of God's light and purpose. In our own lives it can be the same. The slow recognition that God is present in our daily living, and that the powerful hope which Christ brought to earth enfolds us when we take time to listen to the still small voice within. So we journey on unafraid, in the light.

Prayer:

Presence of the living Christ,
be with me to the end of my earthly journeying …
and beyond.

Out of our brokenness
Stories for Easter

Jan Sutch Pickard

In Kippax Uniting Church in Canberra, throughout one Lent, the congregation made a 'kitchen sculpture' on the Communion table. Sunday by Sunday, they brought to church kitchen utensils, pots and pans. New items, still in their packaging, were stowed under the table, to be given as part of starter packs to individuals and families who had been homeless or living in hostels, and who had a chance of a home of their own. But worshippers also brought old utensils, much-used, maybe much loved but superseded – ladles, whisks, measuring jugs, egg timers, enamel mugs, wooden spoons … And these were built up with care into a branching, balancing installation, like a cross, of a very different kind. The theme that Lent, for the congregation, was hospitality – ours, and God's – and the Gospel passages that were read had stories of Jesus receiving hospitality, and offering welcome to those on the margins. The kitchen sculpture was a homely reminder of this.

On Good Friday, as part of a reflective service, I, a visiting storyteller, was invited to stand next to this sculpture, and tell a story inspired by it:

> On a hillside outside Jerusalem the sun beats down. After the bulldozers have left, there is silence. A house has been demolished. A very ordinary house – someone's home. To get near, you will have to walk over broken branches, palm fronds and what's left of the family's olive trees. The leaves are dusty and dying. There was a vine trained over a trellis, making a cool shade for welcoming guests. The trellis is matchwood, the vine torn down. There will be no more grapes.
>
> In the rubble lie smashed crockery, pots and pans, torn curtains, schoolbooks, a computer, shoes, broken glass. So much broken glass.
>
> This was someone's home. Bread was baked here. A family ate together, children played. A working man came back tired at the end of the day. A student daughter returned from college. When neighbours, or strangers, passed by, or stopped at the courtyard gate, friendly voices called 'Salaam Alaikum – peace be upon you! Come! Come.' And folk would come into the yard, and sit down in the shade, and be offered tiny cups of strong sweet black coffee from the pot on the brazier, or glasses of mint tea. Take this cup. The cups are in pieces, the glass is shattered.

This was not an ideal home. There was never enough money to smooth all the rough edges, make everything just so. But there was enough. With its walled garden, an oasis of green in the sunbaked landscape, with its olive trees and fruitful vine and the hospitality of its people, it was a little taste of paradise. A safe place, on a human scale. It has been destroyed – deliberately – as part of a 'collective punishment' by the occupying army.

Children are crying among the rubble. A man and a woman try to comfort each other. People look on in shock. But this is not the only home to be destroyed. There are others close at hand who know what it feels like. They are not saints. Sometimes they lash out. Sometimes they cry out asking where God is, when things like this happen. They are just about hanging on in there – living from day to day with *sumoud* – long-suffering, endurance, steadfastness. Now they reach out to their neighbours in silent compassion. They offer water to drink, shelter from the sun. There will be a place to weep and to sleep, at least tonight, even though hope seems dead.

As the story finished, these words from the Cross were read: *'I promise you that today you will be in Paradise with me'* (Luke 23:43).

Then, in the silence, two people stepped forward, took hold of the cloth over the Communion table, and pulled it hard. The whole sculpture crashed to the ground, clattering and scattering. The silence that followed was shocked and lasted a long time …

On Easter Sunday people of all ages, packing into the church building, discovered the sculpture rebuilt, but transformed. There were some familiar utensils, mingled with new items – heart-shaped cookie cutters, a biscuit tin shaped like a butterfly – the colours bright, sunlight glinting on metal and glass and on the foil around an enormous Easter egg (to be broken by the children and shared in the service).

Again I stood beside the sculpture, which would not be thrown down this time, to tell a story of something fragile and strong:

Happy Easter!

The Easter story is about something surprising, raising big questions, but beautiful too and full of hope. Yesterday I was taken to see your Parliament, which is an amazing building. In the heart of it is a glass case, and in it the text of the apology that was given by the government in 2009 to the Aboriginal people – and next to it is a gift that was their response – a glass *coolamon**. This precious thing is fragile – and yet strong – like reconciliation, like friendship, like hope for the future.

My story is also about glass. But it begins with broken glass. It's a story from the land that we call Holy, and from the city of Bethlehem. There was a terrible time, which was called the Second Intifada, when the Palestinian people were trying to throw off the Israeli Occupation. Tanks rolled into Bethlehem. Stones were thrown. Guns were fired. People were hurt and killed. Houses were demolished. The streets were full of broken glass. It was a mess – like this church when the sculpture was thrown down on Good Friday.

Then the violence stopped for a time. And the curfews were lifted. But life was still hard. Many people in the city were craftsmen – they had made jewellery and pottery and carved olive wood to sell to pilgrims and tourists, who were now afraid to come to the city because of the fighting. So the craftsmen couldn't feed their families or use their skills.

The story says that one man, who was very good at making things, went out of his house when the fighting stopped, and he went round the streets, looking, stopping, picking things up. What was he doing? No one knew. Every day he went out, searching, finding. What? He was picking up broken glass. Glass from house windows and church windows and bottles that had been thrown. Carrying it back to his workshop, he took out his tools, lit his little stove, and worked in secret.

One day he came out of his workshop, and called his family. His little girl came running and he said, 'Hold out your hands' – there was an angel. His son said, 'Me, too, Daddy' – and, look – a star. His wife came forward, smiling, and the maker gave her a dove, a sign of peace.

Here are the things that this craftsman made. Something very surprising. Beautiful ornaments made of broken glass – to hang on your Christmas tree or in your window. An angel – who brings good news; a star – which long ago in Bethlehem was a sign of new life, when Jesus was born; a dove – which reminds us of the peace the risen Jesus brings: Shalom/Salaam.

This Easter, and every Easter: out of our brokenness God can bring good news, new life, the hope of peace.

* 'An Aboriginal container made of wood or bark, used for holding liquids or goods, or carrying a baby'

Love endures
A hymn for Easter Sunday

Jan Sutch Pickard

Love Endures: A hymn for Easter Sunday

This is based on a traditional Easter hymn, which provides the first verse. The new version tells the story verse by verse. It was written for Easter worship on the Isle of Ulva, where recently services have often included storytelling.

Tune: 'Easter hymn', CH 410, and in other hymnbooks

Jesus Christ is risen today, *Alleluia*
Our triumphant holy day, *Alleluia*
Who did once, upon the cross, *Alleluia*
Suffer to redeem our loss, *Alleluia*

Mary came at break of day, *Alleluia*
Found the stone was rolled away, *Alleluia*
Running men, amazed belief, *Alleluia*
Growing hope replacing grief, *Alleluia*

In the garden gapes a cave, *Alleluia*
Weeping at an empty grave, *Alleluia*
Mary, friend of Jesus, stands, *Alleluia*
Aching heart and empty hands, *Alleluia*

Angels throng the brightening air, *Alleluia*
Still the emptiness is there, *Alleluia*
'Gardener, if you took my Lord, *Alleluia*
Tell me where, oh give me word,' *Alleluia*

'Mary' is the word he gives, *Alleluia*
Now she knows that Jesus lives, *Alleluia*
Empty-handed, with full heart, *Alleluia*
Mary runs: the story starts, *Alleluia*

Now let everything that lives, *Alleluia*
Share the hope the Gospel gives, *Alleluia*
Ring, you rocks, and sing, you shores, *Alleluia*
Death's defeated, love endures, *Alleluia.*

Lord of the upper room
A prayer for the first Sunday after Easter

Roddy Cowie

Lord Jesus,
today we remember that you came to the disciples
when they were hiding in the upper room,
afraid to face the world.

We pray for those who lock themselves away,
afraid to face the world:

We pray for those who lock themselves away
because they have been hurt.

We pray for those who lock themselves away
because they feel weak or useless.

We pray for those who lock themselves away
because they are different.

We pray for those who lock themselves away
because they have dangerous enemies.

We pray for those who lock themselves away
because they have done wrong
and cannot bear to face the consequences.

We pray for those who lock themselves away
because they have lost someone they love
and see no way to face the world without them.

We pray for those who lock themselves away
because they have lost hope.

We pray for those we know who are afraid to face the world,
and for the millions we do not know who feel the same way,
and if we know that we are locked away ourselves
then we pray for ourselves too …

And we pray for those who have no choice
but to face pain and hardship –
the sick, the poor and those in trouble …

Lord of the upper room,
be present in the minds of those who need your presence –
be their light,
their friend,
their defender
and their hope.
We ask it in your name.

Roddy Cowie

A litany of laughter
A meditation

Joy Mead

Use different voices.

> *Resurrection is 'a laugh freed forever and ever',*
> wrote the poet Patrick Kavanagh.

See this jester tumble into the ring
in festive mood: to celebrate joy.
Overturn the familiar and go with her
into a looking-glass world
where only the childlike are at home.
She is a storyteller, telling
to anyone who will hear
a story of love and laughter,
an incredible paradox.

Come sing and dance with her;
she's the clown on the floor
with the painted face,
the buffoon, the tragi-comedian.
The fantastic reality
of her message will haunt you
always.

See she plays out her strange part,
contradicts convention, lifts tragedy
into the laughter of heaven,
ushers in a strange, new
wondrous world.

And she'll continue to perform
even when her heart is breaking,
for she is God's fool …

Weeping may linger for the night,
but joy comes with the morning. (Psalm 30, NRSV)

To laugh
is to see sunlight on a spring morning
as it lights up the primroses,

and know that it is good;
to live the moment fully
then let it go.

To laugh
is to know
the joy of eternity.

Weeping may linger for the night,
but joy comes with the morning.

To laugh
is to let that exact,
never to be repeated
movement of muscles
and formation of lines
that is a smile
grow
and spread through the whole
body.
The moment we laugh
our whole bodies
dance for joy.

Weeping may linger for the night,
but joy comes with the morning.

To laugh
is to celebrate the gift of life,
enjoy it and thumb our noses
at those who would destroy
beauty and goodness.

To laugh
is to break the bonds
of evil and oppression.

We laugh, and the words
of the tyrant, the bigot, the bully
no longer threaten us.

Laughter is the sound of joy
heard through a breaking heart.

Weeping may linger for the night,
but joy comes with the morning.

To laugh
is to enter a strange world
of paradox and irony;

to affirm our hope:
that reason and the facts
of the world are not the end
of all things;

to resist the manic search
for one Truth
and the use of violence
to defend that Truth.

To laugh
is to live our questions and
uncertainties;
to have the courage
of our confusions;
to resist the search
for purpose and meaning
and just live
and live justly.

Laughter comes from the reservoir
of our humanity and challenges
or defies injustice, evil, oppression, cruelty.
If laughter is true, it is never empty.
Pure laughter is full
of mercy, compassion, friendship, love.

Weeping may linger for the night,
but joy comes with the morning.

To laugh
is to stand in solidarity
with those who have nothing
to laugh at.

To laugh
is to understand that everything
might be taken away
but we can still laugh,
with Lilith and Sarah,
with Ruth and Naomi,
with Mary and Martha,
with Dorcas and Tabitha,
who knew the laughter
of God.

To laugh
is to light the candle at both ends.
In the darkest night
laughter is prayer.
It's music in the air
and water over stones.

It lifts our human tragedy
into the joy of heaven.

We laugh and we are free.

Suggested songs: 'Over my head', John L. Bell and Graham Maule, from *Love and Anger*, Wild Goose Publications; 'Lord of the dance', Sydney Carter (various songbooks); 'Sing for God's Glory', Kathy Galloway, *Iona Abbey Music Book*, Wild Goose Publications

Ascension and Pentecost
All-age resources and ideas

Janet Lees

Ascension

This piece was written for a sixth-form student who did a charity sky dive.

Blue sky

Blue sky
is hard to imagine
on days when drizzle
dampens everything,
or low clouds
blunt the edges
where earth meets sky,
so minds cannot expand
nor dreams soar upwards.
It is hard to risk
a skyward glance
to check visibility,
when ice crunches
underfoot.
The earth sucks boots down:
it grounds us.
The clearest day
can be shaken
by bits and pieces
burning up in the atmosphere,
raining down on car parks
and back gardens,
reminding us
to keep our heads down.
Only one who knows the skies
inside out
can be companion
in the drizzle,
propelling us skywards
even without a thaw,
to risk the burning,

breathtaking,
lung-bursting
gasp of recognition
that sets us on
our next adventure.

Prayer for Ascensiontide: clinging on

When we go down to the dead
as you did
help us to cling on.

When we soar up to the sky
as you did
help us to cling on.

Whether we are bound for the earth or the sky
take us with you
that wherever you are
we also may be.

Pentecost

Not everything has to be done inside: here are some ideas for all ages to celebrate Pentecost outside. Remember it is better to have a short and memorable activity that everyone can join in than something that goes on too long. Obviously you may need to have a 'wet weather' option available in case of rain.

The wind

Talk about the wind; sing about the wind. 'I love the wind' is a good song to use, also 'Blowing in the wind' – there are many.

Experience the wind: have streamers, bubbles, kites and flags to demonstrate how we cannot see the wind but we can see what it does. Refer to things around you that are 'blowing in the wind'.

Fill yourself up with wind: breathe in deeply. Feel the air fill your lungs. Fill up balloons with air. Do some exercises or circle songs like 'The hokey-cokey'. The message is that the wind is all around us: we cannot see it but we can see what it does.

The Holy Spirit

Talk about the Holy Spirit. Tell the story of Jesus' disciples waiting in Jerusalem for the Holy Spirit (Acts 1:4–9).

There are many images of the Holy Spirit: A dove, pigeon or other birds can be used to recall the Holy Spirit, or the wild goose of the Iona Community. You could use a bird kite. The message: The Holy Spirit comes to us: you cannot see it but you can see what it does and how it changes people who follow Jesus.

Songs for Pentecost

It's easy to make up a short song using the tune 'Frère Jacques', which can be readily sung as a round:

> Fifty days, fifty days,
> watch and wait, watch and wait;
> Holy Spirit's coming, Holy Spirit's coming:
> Pentecost, Pentecost …

Or

> Holy Spirit, Holy Spirit,
> where are you, where are you?
> We are sitting *(standing)* waiting, we are sitting *(standing)* waiting.
> Come down soon, come down soon …

Prayers

Invite participants to make up songs, poems or prayers about the Holy Spirit. Here are a few examples from year 5:

> Dear God,
> thank you for all you have given us:
> for your power deep inside us;
> for being with us every step of the way.

> Dear God,
> thank you for the Holy Spirit:
> helping us on our journey,
> guiding us in daily life,
> inside me and everyone else.

Let us live your love
Harvest prayers

David Osborne

A prayer of thanksgiving

God our Creator,
we offer you our thanks
for your provision of the things we need for life:
food, water, shelter, clothing … each other.

We thank you for those who work the land,
for their skill and patience,
the risks they take and their steady labour;
for those who work to preserve and distribute food;
for the money we have which enables us to buy the things we need;
and for our community life
which enables us to share the produce of the earth.

A prayer of intercession

We pray for those who work,
thinking particularly of farmers, market gardeners and all farm workers …
that they may receive a just reward for what they do.

God, in your mercy,
Hear our prayer.

We pray for those who cannot work,
because of health, disability or lack of opportunity …
that they may know their time and lives are valued.

God, in your mercy,
Hear our prayer.

We pray for those who hunger …
that they may be fed from the plenty the earth provides;
and for all who work to bring relief
to those affected by famine or shortage …
that they may have the support, resources and strength they need.

God, in your mercy,
Hear our prayer.

We pray for those who have great influence over the lives of others,
in government, in the management of industry, finance and commerce,
in the leadership of trade unions,
or because of their great wealth,
or because their words or actions are followed by many …
that they may use their power for the good of all.

God, in your mercy,
Hear our prayer.

We pray for those who struggle to establish justice
where people are oppressed,
or to create opportunities for those who cannot use their skills
or share their insights …
that they may see the fruit of their labour.

God, in your mercy,
Hear our prayer.

We pray for those whose communities are divided by violence or war;
whose health is damaged by the pollution of their soil, water or air;
whose land, livelihoods or homes are damaged by the changing climate …
that they may know your presence in their fear and pain,
and the movement of your Spirit
in the darkness and disorder of the world.

God, in your mercy,
Hear our prayer.
And let us know and live your love.

The granaries of heaven
A Harvest prayer of thanksgiving and concern

Roddy Cowie

Lord God, you created the world
and you saw that it was good.
Today, at harvest time,
we lift our eyes from the pavement and the floor
and look with fresh awareness at the world you gave us.

Open our hearts, good Lord,
to see the riches and the wonder that you give your children:
food to sustain their bodies,
marvellous sights and sounds to feed their minds,
beauty and love to fill their souls.

Open our hearts, good Lord,
until they overflow with happiness and thanks
for all the gifts you give us in your world;
and sweep them clean of petty grumbles
about the little things we would have liked
but that you chose not to give us.

Open our hearts, good Lord,
until – with angels and archangels,
with those who stand across the narrow river on the other side,
and with your faithful servants here on earth in every country –
they overflow with praise.

Open our hearts
to offer you a rich and fitting harvest
not only of our praise, but of our lives,
lived in the way that you intended human lives to be.
We ask it in the name of Jesus Christ, our Lord.

Lord God, at harvest time we pray for those
whose lives are still endured in deserts,
with no hope of harvest.
We pray for those who live in barren places
where the rains fail and the cattle starve.
We pray for them,
and we ask for grace to see the action
that should follow from our prayer –

to see what we can do, and then to do it.
We pray for those who live in devastated and polluted places
ruined by war and human stupidity.
We pray for them,
and we ask for grace to see the action
that should follow from our prayer –
to see what we can do, and then to do it.

We pray for those whose deserts are created by disease –
whose bodies burn with pain or fever,
whose arms are weak,
who could not eat if they had food;
and for those who dedicate their lives to caring for them.
Especially when their caring means risking their own health.
We pray for them,
and we ask for grace to see the action
that should follow from our prayer –
to see what we can do, and then to do it.

We pray for those trapped in the desert of a damaged mind,
caught in the sand of fear,
unable to tell the difference between reality and mirage,
lost and fast losing hope of finding their way to an inhabited city.
We pray for them,
and we ask for grace to see the action
that should follow from our prayer –
to see what we can do, and then to do it.

Lord God, you commanded long ago
that part of every harvest should be set aside
to feed the poor and the foreigner.
Help us to bring the riches of harvest
to your children who have nothing.
We ask it in the name of Jesus Christ, our Lord.

Finally, Lord, we pray for the work of harvest
that you set your church.
Teach us to see in every human spirit
a shoot that you planted,

with all the love that you put into your creation.
Teach us to see in every shoot,
reaching in its own way towards the light
that you created on the first day,
the image of the one who made it.
Help us to understand the patient work
of nurturing precious souls
so that they flourish and shine
and grow towards the perfection
that you long for them to reach.

Give us humility and patience,
forgive us when we fail
and guide our hands and our mouths
to give good care to souls around us in this parish *(community)*
and in all the world,
so that the harvest fills the granaries of heaven
and not one is lost.
We ask it in the name of Jesus Christ, our Lord.

Nature, life and being

A meditative look at climate change, the sacredness of all life and human responsibility

Joy Mead

Be gentle as you walk
on the good earth,
our home and lifegiver.
Touch with kindness
all that has being
and shares with you
this sacred space.

Smell the subtle scent
of bluebells in the spring;
hear the summer wind
in the grass, feel it
light on your back;
touch the trees,
sense their nearness.
Know the fragility
of wondrous plants.

Listen with care
to the blackbird's song,
the lark's morning joy
and the cuckoo's haunting call.
Hold in your heart
these sounds of life.

Let the precious wetness
of falling rain baptise you.
Breathe deeply, fill your lungs
with the air that keeps you
alive; understand the need
to sustain its breathability.

Be still and connect
in the silence
what you are
with what you value.

Never overvalue your own significance
nor undervalue it. Know yourself
one small, vulnerable part.
Feel your feet on the earth
and know the joy of your place
in the natural world.

Know our human need
for beauty.
We fall in love with all life
in beautiful places.

Rediscover your sense of wonder
and share it with others –
it might yet be our salvation.

Give attention to life's littleness –
contemplate what it means
to honour the small things –
the seeds and sunlight –
that sustain our wider being.

Learn to simply be and live wholly
where you are, and who you are
and who you are with.

You, you're another me;
me … I'm another you.
We're neither subject
nor object. We're one
with each other
and the world.
On this sense of equality
our survival may depend.

Love life as you live it.
Don't try to outdo it.
Let beauty break through
your frantic need to do.

We're the between people,
the people on the edge
of catastrophe.
Our obsessive doing
may be our destruction.
But we have, it seems,
one last chance to save
ourselves and honour
our beautiful earth.

Look at your own hands,
small but with infinite possibilities.
Big problems need small solutions.
Put out your hand to those who have gone.
Their wisdom and faithfulness stays with us.

Be prophetic and creative;
reach out to those
who are to come
with love in your heart.

Listen, feel, touch and smell;
think and imagine –
these are sacred acts.
Real life is what it is
not what you might be told it is.
Listen to the earth
and life as you meet it.

Watch and never turn away.
Discern what is needful.
Seek to overcome the greedy child
who is inside each one of us
and would take to itself
what belongs to all.

We can no longer sleep unaware
nor be silent while others sleep.
May the sound of our own voices
disturb our foolish slumber.

Awake and see!
Awake and tell what you see!
Awake and seek
a sustainable and fairer future
for all life on earth.

A blessing for a new car

David Coleman

This liturgy is for a 'new' used car too, of course.

The wording could be adapted and divided up among more than two people (e.g. a family).

Opening responses:

Leader: Our help is in the name of the Lord.
Driver: Who has made heaven and earth.

Leader: The Lord be with you.
Driver: And also with you.

Leader: A blessing on your driving forth.
Driver: And on my turning home.

Leader: Lord, we do not know the Way.
Driver: Jesus says: 'I am the Way.'

Leader: We get in, and prepare to drive.

In the beginning, God said, 'Let there be light.'

(Driver turns ignition on.)

And there was light, and God saw
that the light was good …

(Driver puts car in gear.)

(Drive a little way – up to a viewpoint, and park.)

So here we are in this new vehicle,
with so many possibilities.

And costs. Not just to us.
Its use, as we burn fuel,
or consume energy,
even the limited life of our batteries,
will cost the earth.
So we ask for wisdom
to drive discerningly and economically.

A blessing for a new car 155

Its use will save time, hassle, stress and aggravation.
So we will drive with great thanksgiving.

Its use may bring us and others into danger.
So we will look to drive in safety and watchfulness.

It will bring us to new places and perspectives.
So we will always seek guidance in how to fruitfully interpret what we encounter.

And as we will not always drive alone,
we ask for the blessing of peaceful passengers.

Reflection:

The 'traditional' Bible reading for blessing a car is Acts chapter 8, verses 26–40, where Philip runs alongside the Ethiopian in his chariot, and the Ethiopian offers him a lift. And the two of them drive along the road together, talking about God's Word. Today the Ethiopian would probably be charged for reading while driving – or indeed using his smartphone. Well, maybe he had a chauffeur!

What we have in this passage is the special sort of conversation that does happen in a vehicle as folk share the bumps and twists and turns of a journey, while both needing to keep alert.

But I'd like to take our chat a bit further. Because the relationship of the Bible with wheeled vehicles is quite extensive.

First of all, a question: if this car were in the Bible, when would it be like a wagon or cart, as in a humble, everyday vehicle that's used to carry supplies and groceries, like here in Genesis 45:21: *'Jacob's sons agreed to do what the king had said. And Joseph gave them wagons and food for their trip home, just as the king had ordered'*? And when would it be like a chariot – comfortable, flashy and dignified?

Chariots, of course, also suggest an aggressive or offensive capability.

We bear in mind that this vehicle is capable of travelling faster than any in the history of the world, up until about half a century ago. Less than a lifetime.

And because being surrounded by all this power amplifies, rather than hides, your mood, what you do with it does, and should, put you under the spotlight. Are we different people when we drive?

Remember how when Jehu's chariot was glimpsed in the distance, people recognised it immediately, because of his driving style: *'The driving is like the driving of Jehu, son of Nimshi, for he driveth furiously'* (2 Kings 9:20).

There is even a suggestion in the Bible – and it's one that every driver needs to be mindful of – that vehicles are a last resort. In Exodus 25, carrying the Ark of the Covenant on foot is the most holy mode of transport. Certainly the Philistines get themselves into trouble when, instead of shouldering the Ark, they use an ox cart. So, don't use the car when the appropriate thing is to walk. But that, of course, is a matter of discernment.

There is the exhilaration, euphoria and real joy of motoring – into the sunrise or sunset, with the windows open or the top down, with the heady scent of summer in the air and the wind through our hair, with a favourite song on the radio – and a good clear road ahead. The woman in the Song of Songs (6:11), no less, says:

I went down to see if blossoms were on the walnut trees,
grapevines and fruit trees.
But in my imagination
I was suddenly riding on a glorious chariot ...

Which brings us to the sense in which a chariot is a vehicle of God, or of the angels. A chariot carries angels on the top of Noah's Ark. And a fiery chariot transports the prophet Elijah to the domain of God.

And what else is an internal combustion vehicle but a *'chariot of concealed fire'*?

There's the lovely vision in Zechariah 6 of *four chariots coming from between two bronze mountains. The first chariot was pulled by red horses, and the second by black horses; the third chariot was pulled by white horses, and the fourth by spotted grey horses. 'Sir,' I asked the angel. 'What do these stand for?'*

Then he explained, 'These are the four winds of heaven, and now they are going out, after presenting themselves to the Lord of all the earth ...'

But if your vehicle is electric, then consider this: the power and convenience does not come at no cost at all, and does not make you better than other drivers, though we may give thanks that you do less harm, in the sense that, via turbines of one sort or another, you are powered by the wind, the breath, the Spirit, which blows where it will (John 3:8). Give thanks for the freedom this gives, and pray for the grace to use it wisely, for justice, for joy. But remember that to generate electricity, like it or not, we still largely use nuclear power, which equips weapons of mass destruction. So commit yourself anew to drive ahead for peace.

Zechariah 6 again:

When they had gone on their way, he shouted to me, 'Those that have gone to the country in the north will do what the Lord's Spirit wants them to do there.'

Here, in the country in the north, living our daily life, trying to follow the Way, and using the gift of this vehicle, it does come down to putting ourselves in God's hands.

A traditional blessing for a car:

Let us pray.

Lord God, lend a willing ear to our prayers, and bless this vehicle.

Direct your holy angels to accompany it, that they may free those who ride in it from all dangers and always guard them.

And just as by your servant Philip you gave faith and grace to the Ethiopian as they sat in his chariot reading the sacred Word, so give guidance to your servants in navigating the way of salvation.

Grant that, aided by your grace, we may, after all the joys and sorrows of this journey through life, find eternal joys, through Christ our Lord.

Amen

The car is anointed with fragrant oil.

Seven days

Stories & reflections for the World Week for Peace in Palestine & Israel

Jan Sutch Pickard &
members of the Iona Community

Introduction: 'Bridges not walls'

These pieces were written for the 2016 World Week for Peace in Palestine and Israel (WWPPI), which takes place in September. The theme of the 2016 week was 'Bridges not walls'.

As an ecumenical movement of women and men of different ages, backgrounds and nationalities, the Iona Community has learned a lot about the blocks to justice, the barriers that confront us as we try to walk in God's Way. Some of these are of our own making. But we've also learned quite a bit about building bridges, and making connections.

Some of us have worked for many years in the Middle East, others have been challenged and changed by a single visit. Three of the contributors to Seven Days have served as Ecumenical Accompaniers on the WCC's programme in Israel/Palestine, and draw on that experience here.

Though we come from different traditions and disciplines and have different styles of writing, all of us, as members of the Community, share its Justice and Peace Commitment, which includes these words: *'We believe that the Gospel commands us to seek peace founded on justice and that costly reconciliation is at the heart of the Gospel. We believe that work for justice, peace and an equitable society is a matter of extreme urgency'* (from the Rule of the Iona Community).

That urgency includes the knowledge that oppression is a daily experience for many of our sisters and brothers. In the face of injustice, we can feel helpless. Confronted by the enormity of the Separation Barrier, for instance, and when the possibility of meaningful action is blocked – when we see people on both sides dehumanised – our hearts demand, 'Where is God in all this?' But many of us are, as individuals and Iona Community Family Groups, signatories to the Kairos Britain document, which affirms God's presence in these hard places and declares that God's time for justice is now. That is the belief underlying the following prayer, written for this year's WWPPI. May God use what we offer here to enable reflection and action, to connect many gatherings, many places and many people like yourself, during these seven days.

Prayer: Bridges not walls

God-with-us, you sit down in our midst.
Nothing can separate us from your love –
not towering concrete walls
or the deep darkness between searchlights;
not distance from friends
or despair in our hearts
that the world's wrongs cannot be changed.
You are with our brothers crowded at the checkpoint,
with our sisters witnessing for peace:
you sit down in our midst.
Born into poverty, to displaced people living under occupation,
you shared our human lives,
and we know that your love can never be contained
by the walls of separation.
You sit down in our midst, God-with-us.
Amen

Jan Sutch Pickard

Day 1: Pilgrims in divided lands

1961. My seven-year-old eyes saw seven days of wonder.

We flew on an ancient plane, rattling with wartime tales, into Beirut, to wait on plastic seats in the heat until another plane was ready. We flew again, so close to the earth that I saw the shepherds and their herds on the hills where Jesus walked. We were on the far side of Jordan, low over the Golan Heights, above the Syrian Sea. Bound for the West Bank, Israel's Galilee was forbidden.

Jerusalem smelt of bread and drains in its narrow, stepped streets. We went into the buildings, down stairs to the centuries of Jesus. The streets were thronged. Veiled ladies, weighted with cheap coins, carried pitchers on their heads with the grace of the poor. A girl my age passed in a dress made from a sack. The friars gave out free bread daily to grasping hands: we stood behind them with the voyeurism of the visitor.

Holy Sepulchre had marble steps rounded by centuries of wear. There was a crack in the seat in the place that Jesus died, and deeper cracks in human concord. And the gleam of the golden mosque was forbidden to us, by a boundary stronger than walls.

We went to pray, and prayer raised questions.

At Lazarus' tomb, by steps greasy from centuries of candles, sat a boy covered in open sores and the flies whose ancestors stung Jesus on the cross. Curious, he watched our party come, then go. Is he now in Abraham's bosom? On the road to Bethlehem, Bedouin sheltered in caves; on the road to Jericho we sheltered from the sun under fig trees heavy with leaves and fruit, then went down to the depths of the hot earth, with no fear of robbers on our bus. Jordan was a small river that autumn before the rains, easily crossed by shepherd and soldier.

Back in Jerusalem we passed to the Potter's Field in No-Man's-Land. The wait at the crossing bored me and I slipped through to sit on a bollard. 'Come back,' they called, urgently. I was embarrassed for them: that Israeli soldier patrolling the walls, had he heard? That they thought he would shoot me! We went at last under white flag and watched the work and bought the pots amid sun-crinkled smiles.

It was the chance visit to feed a lifetime's imagination, a link to the living Jesus. That included the land's divisions. The Potter's Field was bought in blood, at the cost of God, and it buried the stories of stranger and neighbour. A few years later, that empty territory was overrun, the people fled and checkpoints ended. A road was bulldozed through it. Divisions were overcome, and created.

We build our walls through the lands and tales of others, where we should tread lightly, for we tread upon dreams. Of fear, forced movement, fragile hopes, and the need for daily bread and justice.

Scripture

Jesus knew their thoughts and said to them, 'Every kingdom divided against itself will be ruined, and every city or household divided against itself will not stand. If Satan drives out Satan, he is divided against himself. How then can his kingdom stand? And if I drive out demons by Beelzebub, by whom do your people drive them out? So then, they will be your judges. But if I drive out demons by the Spirit of God, then the kingdom of God has come upon you.' (Matthew 12:25–28, NIV)

Prayer

Creator Lord
of the unclaimed place
and of clashing claims,
of no one's land where some have homes,
in danger zones,
in human souls, in nations' claims:
we are all guilty.
We build barriers to hide what we fear to see,
we draw lines in other people's hearts,
we trample underfoot what others hold dear,
we wear wounds unhealed with anger,
we defend ourselves from other people's rights.
Drive out the demons that divide neighbours.

Jesus,
in the land where your feet were tired,
where you carried the oppressor's burden,
broke the chains of the prisoners,
demolished walls, made wounded lives blossom,
and set our hearts free
to turn and to serve:
may you be the potter
in our lives' neutral zones;
in divided land,
may justice return.

Spirit of hope,
may those who build houses live in them,
those who plant olive trees harvest them,
may they shelter under fig trees,
give water to strangers,
tell stories to children,
keep Covenant with God.
As we honour the graves of our neighbours
may we face those we fear,
cry justice for the oppressed,
tell of love without end:
may peace flourish till the moon fails.

Rosemary Power

Day 2: Into Galilee

In October 1990 I had the immense privilege of spending almost two weeks in the Holy Land. We were a group of six – originally intended to be 25 or so – Scottish 'church leaders', but the visit was scaled down as people withdrew in the wake of the Iraqi invasion of Kuwait in August that year.

The kaleidoscope of memories is vivid still: the challenging meetings we had with so many interesting and impressive people, including (now Archbishop) Elias Chacour at Ibillin; Hanan Ashrawi, politician and activist; and Naim Ateek, founder of Sabeel Liberation Theology Centre. We visited the tragic ruins at the beautiful deserted village of Bir'im, Chacour's birthplace, near the Lebanon border, as vigilant helicopters buzzed overhead. I was moved to tears, a rare occurrence for me, I confess, by the terrible conditions at the Jabalia refugee camp in Gaza. Then, later on, as we experienced kind hospitality in a home in the Jalazone refugee camp near Ramallah, I gradually realised that another experience, of stinging eyes, was because the neighbourhood had been tear-gassed.

We were celebrating Communion beside the Church of the Multiplication at Tabgha on the shore of the Sea of Galilee – fishing boats out on the lake, dragonflies and birdsong all around – when reality suddenly intervened and the tranquillity was shattered by a couple of deafeningly loud, low-flying Israeli jets.

But clearest of all, returning to me again and again, and drawing me back to visit Palestine-Israel once more – before too long, I hope – is the recollection of the meeting we had in Nazareth with the mayor, Tawfiq Ziad. He embodied commitment, courage and compassion. He described himself as 'communist, but three-quarters Orthodox'. He told us how his wife had been imprisoned and his daughter grievously injured by the Israeli authorities because of their pursuit of justice for the Palestinians. Both poet and politician, a member of the Knesset and an inveterate campaigner for human rights and social and political change, he died in 1994 in a head-on collision in the Jordan Valley on his way home from Jericho after welcoming Yasser Arafat back from exile. When we met, he movingly shared with us his hopes and vision for the future. His words will live with me always: *'I dream of the day when there will be bread in every mouth, a smile on every face, and a rose in every hand.'*

Scripture

'But after I am raised up, I will go ahead of you, leading the way to Galilee.'
(Mark 14:28, *The Message*)

Prayer

God of generosity and grace,
help us to hold fast to the vision and values of your kingdom
and to trust in your loving purpose,
your promise that all things are being made new.
God of justice and joy,
help us to be faithful to our calling to walk in the footsteps of Jesus,
to be people of hospitality, integrity, justice and compassion.
Amen

Norman Shanks

Day 3: 'Dead easy'

Gideon is a man who I would guess is in his mid-forties. A kindly man with a friendly demeanour, but he is carrying a big gun. We Ecumenical Accompaniers meet up with Gideon at the agricultural gate to the north of the village of Jayyous, where he is on duty as a reservist with the Israeli Defence Force. For three weeks every year he serves as a soldier with the IDF. Today he is on duty at the north gate and because there is very little traffic going through the gate we get a chance to talk to him.

The gate is in the Separation Barrier, which winds its way from north to south, dividing Palestinians from Israelis. At many points it veers eastwards from the 'Green Line' – the internationally agreed demarcation between Israeli and Palestinian territory – so it also divides Palestinians from their land. Jayyous is a farming village and seventy percent of its land is now on the 'Israeli' side. There are agricultural gates to the north and south of Jayyous, open for just an hour three times a day, allowing farmers with permits to pass through gates in the Separation Barrier to access their land on the other side. However in 2008, when I meet Gideon there, only twenty percent of Jayyous farmers are in possession of permits.

To obtain a permit a farmer needs to produce an ID card, a current permit, proof of connection to the land, a map of the land in question, a certificate of inheritance and proof that the land has not been sold and still belongs to the applicant. And there is no appeal against refusal. Obtaining a permit is a bureaucratic nightmare. 'Permits mean losing land step by step,' according to our hydrologist friend in the village.

Gideon's mother, he tells us, was killed by a sixteen-year-old suicide bomber in Tel Aviv. 'Who is more important for you than your mother?' But he bears no grudges against the Palestinians per se, he tells us, acknowledging that there is suffering on both sides in this long-running conflict. I'm drawn to Gideon, who seems a compassionate man. I feel for him when he tells me about an injury he suffered while hot-air ballooning for a hobby.

But his parting remark really floors me. 'It's dead easy,' he tells us, 'for Palestinians to get and renew their permits.' How is it possible for a seemingly kind and considerate person to have such a totally misconceived view of life in this Palestinian village? Sadly it is probably symptomatic of much Israeli ignorance about life in the West Bank.

Scripture

'There is no good faith or loyalty, no acknowledgment of God in the land … Want of knowledge has been the ruin of my people. As you have rejected knowledge, so will I reject you …' (Hosea 4:1b, 6, REB)

Prayer

Open our eyes, God, to a world of inequality.
Open our eyes to injustice far away and close at hand.
Disturb us, challenge us, remind us:
'The only thing necessary for the triumph of evil
is for good men to do nothing.'
And, when we find it 'dead easy' not to see
what is life-denying – then, living God,
open our eyes. Amen

Colin Douglas

Day 4: Standing up to be counted

It seems to me that, if Israel's illegal occupation of Palestine is to end, it is vitally important that the Israeli people themselves stand up to challenge their own government.

That is what 'Women in Black' are doing in West Jerusalem every Friday: standing as an act of witness.

Women in Black grew out of the 'Black Sash' movement in apartheid South Africa, and started in Israel in 1988. I joined them in 1990 and stood with them whenever I could be in Jerusalem, until my last time in Israel/Palestine in 2010.

We started Women in Black Scotland in Edinburgh in 2001, when the UK invaded Afghanistan, and have not missed a Saturday since: 1-2pm at the east end of Princes Street – do join us!

We are part of a worldwide network of women committed to peace with justice, opposed to injustice, war, militarism and other forms of violence.

An important focus is challenging the policies of our own governments. We're not an organisation but a means of communication with a simple, effective form of action.

The Women in Black in Israel stand in West Jerusalem on Fridays from 1-2pm. The majority are women, of all ages, but men do sometimes join them. Most are Jewish – as Palestinians from East Jerusalem and the Occupied West Bank are usually not permitted to cross into West Jerusalem. They are often joined by visitors from all over the world.

In the days when I was there we received a variety of responses from the public – we were spat at by passers-by, and one day a man pushed one of the women right over. We were shouted at by Orthodox young men and chanted at from across the street by 'Women in White', who support the settlements. But sometimes passers-by brought us cakes and biscuits – and once we were handed flowers!

As the Occupation continues and becomes more draconian, there is much more abuse – horrible things are shouted from passing drivers (it is an advantage not to understand too much Hebrew!). But the Women in Black say, 'If we were not important they would ignore us.'

And so they still stand every week, holding up their signs: 'End the Occupation'.

Scripture

The Lord says, 'The land is mine and you are but aliens and my tenants.' (Leviticus 25:23, NIV)

Prayer

God, you have given us hearts to love and minds to think:
give us the desire for change,
and show us the way to help make change happen.
We pray for those who are prepared to stand up
and be hated and called traitors by their own people.
We pray for the Women in Black at their vigils,
and for the young Israelis who refuse to do compulsory military service –
the 'Refuseniks' – who may be imprisoned,
and for the soldiers who, having served,
now speak out, 'Breaking the Silence'. Amen

Runa Mackay

Day 5: Let justice roll down like waters

We've been sitting on a bus on the Allenby/King Hussein Bridge over the River Jordan for hours, waiting for permission to cross the Israeli 'border' into the West Bank, wondering whether this time our story of being tourists in the Holy Land will be believed by the suspicious border guards of the Occupation.

The water of the River Jordan is an invisible, polluted, saline trickle, only 4% of what it was 70 years ago.[1] Up to the end of the British Mandate it probably flowed as freely as it did when Jesus was baptised. The water of the Jordan has since been diverted by Israel to the Naqab/Negev desert to turn the land green and habitable – for some. The Palestinian Bedouin, who were already living sustainably in the desert, are being evicted. The village of Al Araqib has been demolished well over 100 times (2019 figure). Each time the inhabitants return and rebuild.

The diversion of the River Jordan was an iconic act of Zionist engineering, initiated before the state of Israel was founded in 1948 and completed in 1964, to 'redeem the land for the Jews'. Most who lived in the catchment of this essential resource have been dispossessed. While Lebanon, Syria and Jordan also border the River Jordan, Israel commandeers 70% of its water. Occupied Palestine has no access.[2]

Water is a source of daily anxiety for Palestinians. In Gaza, Israeli bombing campaigns which destroyed the infrastructure, the continuing blockade and constant power cuts make a reliable water supply impossible. In the West Bank, with its aquifers deep under the limestone hills, water sources are taken over by settlements, or village wells deliberately polluted.[3] *'Throughout the summer months, hundreds of thousands of Palestinians in the West Bank suffer a severe shortage of water for personal consumption, bathing, cleaning, livestock and irrigation. The severe shortage violates basic human rights, including the right to health, decent housing, equality and the benefit of natural resources. All this is the result of the Israeli policy, in place since 1967, which is based on unfair allocation of water resources in the West Bank.'* (B'Tselem website)

This story also comes from B'Tselem, the Israeli organisation which monitors and challenges the Occupation: *'On 14 June 2016, despite the 104°F heat in the Jordan Valley, Israeli authorities seized a tractor on which Palestinians depend to carry water to their flocks and delivered demolition orders for spring water reservoirs that are vital to al-Malih Palestinian community. This conduct clearly illustrates Israel's routine abuse of its power against Palestinians in the Jordan Valley, exacerbating the existing water shortage caused by the fact Israel does not allow them to connect to the water supply.'*

The solution to the ecological disaster of the Jordan River valley depends on the framing of the problem. There have been various initiatives, from the World Bank's heavy engineering 'Red Sea-Dead Sea Water Conveyance Project', through to the NGO EcoPeace Middle East's sustainable management-based 'Jordan River Rehabilitation Programme'. These initiatives, it is claimed, are evidence that solutions must be based on co-operation. However, to Palestinian environmental and human rights groups and hydrologists, these projects are flawed because by 'co-operating' with the Israeli occupation, they perpetuate it. This leads to an acceptance of, rather than a challenge to, Israel's illegal dispossession of Palestinian water rights. Any sustainable solution must be based on an equal right to water for Israelis and Palestinians: that means an end to the Occupation and water fairly shared.

Scripture

Jesus came from Nazareth in Galilee and was baptised in the Jordan by John. No sooner had he come up out of the water than he saw the heavens torn apart, and the Spirit, like a dove, descending on him. And a voice came from heaven, 'You are my Son, the Beloved; my favour rests on you.' Immediately afterwards, the Spirit drove him out into the wilderness. And he stayed in the wilderness forty days, being tempted by Satan; and he was with the wild beasts, and the angels ministered to him. Now after John was arrested, Jesus came into Galilee, preaching the good news of the kingdom of God ... saying 'The time is fulfilled, and the kingdom of God is at hand; repent and believe the good news.' (Mark 1:9–15, Jerusalem Bible)

Reflection/prayer

In Jesus' baptism we witness the fulfilment of Isaiah's prophecy: 'Behold, my servant, whom I uphold ... I have put my Spirit upon him; he will bring forth justice to the nations.' (Isaiah 42:1, ESV)

Following Jesus into the wilderness, we reflect on the universal human need for water; our feeling of helplessness in the face of the dispossession of Palestinians from this life source; the dehumanising ideology of Zionism, and our temptation, in turn, to dehumanise Israelis for the sins of their state. May our solidarity and concern for justice both spring from love for our fellow human beings.

Grant us that same Spirit which descended on Jesus in the Jordan: to be servants of God and bringers of justice.

The time has come! The moment of truth – the kingdom of God is at hand. In our prayers and in our actions, we hope for the transformation of human relationships that is repentance, through the decolonisation of the water, land and people of Palestine, so that oppressors and oppressed may become sisters and brothers.

Let justice roll down like waters, and righteousness like an ever-flowing stream. (Amos 5:24, ESV)

Eurig Scandrett

Notes:

1. Palestinian landscape and the Israeli–Palestinian conflict, Jad Isaac & Jane Hilal: www.tandfonline.com/doi/abs/10.1080/00207233.2011.582700?journalCode=genv20

2. Palestinian landscape and the Israeli–Palestinian conflict, Jad Isaac & Jane Hilal: www.tandfonline.com/doi/abs/10.1080/00207233.2011.582700?journalCode=genv20

3. See the film *The Iron Wall,* by Mohammed Alatar, and documentation by B'Tselem, the Israeli Information Centre for Human Rights in the Occupied Territories (http://www.btselem.org)

Day 6: Refugees twice over

In December 2008 I was one of a team of five international human rights observers based in East Jerusalem, working with the World Council of Churches Ecumenical Accompaniment Programme. At 4am on a Sunday morning we were phoned by our contact with news we had been half expecting: a Palestinian couple, Abu and Fawzieh Al Kurd, who lived in the Sheikh Jarrah neighbourhood, were being evicted from their home of 52 years. We knew that Fawzieh was attending her seriously sick husband.

By the time we arrived, the area had been declared a military zone and been cordoned off by a detachment of Israeli soldiers and military police. Members of the International Solidarity Movement, who had been camping on the verandah, were arrested and later deported. The Al Kurds and several other families in Sheikh Jarrah had been resisting eviction for a number of years, first when a group of Jewish settlers from the Yemen claimed ownership of the land. That claim was shown in the courts to be without legal foundation, but the state of Israel refused to re-zone the land. Meanwhile other settlers began to infiltrate the neighbourhood.

On their return from a hospital visit in Jordan in 2001 the Al Kurds found a recently completed extension to their home occupied by a settler family – which, seven years later, was still there. Now, on that December morning they had taken over the rest of the house. Those to whom it had been home were reduced to the indignity of living in a tent on a neighbour's land.

Their experience has been shared by many. There have been hundreds of evictions and house demolitions in East Jerusalem in recent years, part of a strategy to transform Jerusalem into an Israeli city, which involves the forced expulsion of hundreds of Palestinian families from their homes.

On the day of the eviction Abu Al Kurd was admitted to hospital. He died a week later. Fawzieh now lives with her family in another part of the city, although even there she is not secure. She reflects that she has been a refugee twice over: once in the 1950s when, as a girl, she had been evicted with her family from their home in West Jerusalem following the creation of the state of Israel. Now this …

As we left the scene that day we recalled her generous hospitality whenever we visited and the words of defiance on the large banner stretched across their verandah: 'We will never leave our home.'

Scripture

Isaiah of Jerusalem (8th century BCE) said to his contemporaries:

Woe betide those who add house to house
and join field to field
until everyone else is displaced
and you are left as sole inhabitants of the land.
God looked for justice but found bloodshed,
for righteousness, but heard cries of distress.

(Isaiah 5:8,7b, REB)

Poem

There was a crucifixion in Jerusalem
today.
Under cover of darkness they came,
long before dawn,
armed to the teeth;
unjust sentence already passed
separating a family
from their home of fifty years.
Usual suspects gather:
soldiers lounge at barriers,
smoking, drinking coffee;
friends, neighbours watch
from a distance,
seething with impotent rage;
black-clad religious
pass to and fro;
notable absentees.
Some time after noon
a word from the cross –

the indomitable Fawzieh,
wheelchair-bound husband
by her side,
voices vehement protest,
passionate faith that
right will prevail.
Still soldiers watch
waiting for the end.
There was a crucifixion in Jerusalem
today.

Warren Bardsley

Day 7: Bread

Maryam took yeast, mixed it with flour and water, and set it to rise.

The yeast was bought from the nearby town of Aqraba. It was the only ingredient that came from outside Yanoun. The grain grown in the flat fields on the valley bottom was harvested and stored here until it could be ground by the mobile mill that visits the village. The water came from the village well, in the olive grove at the foot of the hill. She gave the dough twelve hours to rise. Then, as the children were going to school next door, she went into the bake-house and sat down by the *taboon*.

I have been sitting with her for the last hour, watching her at work and talking gently, as we waited for the flatbread to bake.

A *taboon* is an earth-oven, a depression in the ground, lined with stones that hold the heat, and fired up with the dross from the olive-press, which makes very good fuel, the embers of which are piled over the domed cover of the *taboon* to give out a smouldering heat and bake the loaves right through.

Maryam is married to Murad, a farmer who herds sheep and goats, has olive trees and some land under plough – in every case less than before the settlements were built and the outposts appeared on the hilltops around the village. They have six children, and also Murad's housebound mother to feed. Maryam talks as she works, about her hopes for her children's education, her fears of the settlers and for the future of the village.

She takes the lid from the *taboon*, and the heat rises into the dark little hut, in which flour dust and smoke dance in a ray of sun. With deft, floured hands, Maryam scoops some of the soft dough from the bowl, and places it on a floured tray, flattens it to the shape of the tray. Then, as she lifts it up using both hands, it starts to stretch. Deftly she keeps it in motion so that it doesn't tear and swiftly drapes it on the hot stones in the *taboon*. On goes the lid, and we wait again, and talk.

I look at her beautiful tired face, which I cannot photograph, out of respect. And, with equal respect, watch the growing pile of bread she is making – and makes every day – to feed her family. I'm given a crusty, fragrant, still-warm loaf to take home for my household. This is Sunday morning. This is a sacrament.

Scripture

Give us today our daily bread. (Matthew 6:11, REB)

The Lord … deals out justice to the oppressed, feeds the hungry and sets the prisoner free. (Psalm 146, 7, 8, REB)

Prayer

With-us God, you came to share our human lives
in Bethlehem – 'the house of bread'.
We pray for those who bake bread and break it
on both sides of the wall of separation:
Jewish families gathered for the Shabbat meal,
Christian and Muslim Palestinians
sharing flatbread fresh from the *taboun*.
You are Living Bread, broken that all might be fully alive,
so we pray for the day when all your children
will be free to share their daily bread together, in peace.
Amen

Jan Sutch Pickard

Some websites and resources

Breaking the Silence (Israeli soldiers talk about the Occupied Territories): http://www.breakingthesilence.org.il

B'Tselem (The Israeli Information Centre for Human Rights in the Occupied Territories): http://www.btselem.org

Ecumenical Accompaniment Programme in Palestine and Israel (EAPPI): https://www.oikoumene.org/en/what-we-do/eappi

International Solidarity Movement: https://palsolidarity.org/

Iona Community: www.iona.org.uk

Kairos Britain: www.kairosbritain.org.uk

Sabeel Liberation Theology Centre: http://sabeel.org/

Women in Black: http://womeninblack.org

World Week for Peace in Palestine and Israel: https://www.oikoumene.org/en/press-centre/events/world-week-of-peace-in-palestine-and-israel

Sources and acknowledgements

THE HOLY BIBLE, NEW INTERNATIONAL VERSION® NIV® Copyright © 1973,1978, 1984 by International Bible Society® Used by permission. All rights reserved worldwide.

Scripture quotations from THE MESSAGE. Copyright © by Eugene H. Peterson 1993, 1994, 1995, 1996, 2000, 2001, 2002. Used by permission of NavPress. All rights reserved. Represented by Tyndale House Publishers, Inc.

Scripture quotations taken from the Revised English Bible, copyright © Cambridge University Press and Oxford University Press 1989. All rights reserved.

From The Jerusalem Bible © 1966 by Darton Longman & Todd Ltd and Doubleday and Company Ltd.

The Holy Bible, English Standard Version® (ESV®) Copyright © 2001 by Crossway, a publishing ministry of Good News Publishers. All rights reserved.

Note: The names of people in some of the stories in this resource have been changed to preserve confidentiality.

Racial justice
A reflection and a prayer

Iain & Isabel Whyte

Reflection: resources to draw on

> 'We have been concerned with the more subtle and much discussed concept of racism referred to as institutional racism which (in the words of Dr Robin Oakley) can influence police service delivery "not solely through the deliberate actions of a small number of bigoted individuals, but through a more systematic tendency that could unconsciously influence police performance generally".'[1]

These were the words of the Macpherson Report in 1999, on the police investigation of the murder of the black teenager Stephen Lawrence in 1993. The same questions continue to be asked today, as the family of Sheku Bayoh from Sierra Leone seek answers to his death, after a police arrest in Fife, Scotland in May 2015.

To understand racism today in Scotland, in Britain, in Europe, we need to accept and confront the fundamental truth that it is institutional as much as personal. As the Macpherson Report stated:

> 'Racism in general terms consists of conduct or words or practices which disadvantage or advantage people because of their colour, culture, or ethnic origin. In its more subtle form it is as damaging as in its overt form.'[2]

We can all identify and respond to the prejudiced language or behaviour of individuals. These can be challenged, although that often takes courage. There is legislation in the UK that makes *'incitement to racial hatred'* a criminal offence. But to name, identify and challenge racism that is at the heart of many of our institutions (and the police are far from alone) is much more complex. Yet it is urgent for the good of our society. The recent increase in Islamophobia, as a reaction to terrorism, carries with it not just a distortion of a major world religion, but often a blanket racism aimed at any who make up a multicultural society. What then are the resources in our own faith tradition that we can draw on?

The prophetic tradition of the Old Testament has much to assist us. The prophets knew the story of racial discrimination and oppression against Hebrews in Egypt, and so the Jewish Torah (the Law) at that early stage incorporated the warning:

> *'You shall not oppress a resident alien; you know the heart of an alien, for you yourselves were aliens in the land of Egypt.'* (Exodus 23:9, NRSV)

The prophets were to develop this in terms of looking at other nations, when Israel took possession of the Promised Land. Corporate injustice, corporate discrimination, corporate oppression were condemned, as was national zenophobia. Amos started his prophesy by detailing the sins of the nations round about, but before the people of Israel and Judah stopped cheering he warned them that as God's people they bore a heavier responsibility for their national crimes:

> *'Hear this word that the Lord has spoken against ... the whole family that I brought out of the land of Egypt: You only have I known of all the families of the earth; therefore I will punish you for all your iniquities.'* (Amos 3:1–2, NRSV)

> *For lo, the Lord is coming out of his place, and will come down and tread upon the high places of the earth. Then the mountains will melt under him and the valleys will burst open, like wax near the fire, like waters poured down a steep place. All this for the transgressions of Jacob and for the sins of the house of Israel.* (Micah 1:3–4, NRSV)

We need to remind those who defend the way in which the state of Israel treats its Palestinian citizens and those under occupation that their own sacred history contains these same warnings. But at a personal level we all have to recognise our capacity for racism. That point was continually made by the late Trevor Huddleston, mentor of Desmond Tutu and indefatigable opponent of the evil of apartheid, where, as in the southern American states in pre-civil rights time, racism was institutionalised by law.

South Africa has now overthrown apartheid, and civil rights is officially the policy of the United States. But, as in Britain, the poison of racism is by no means purged from the system. There is a continuing rearguard action by many white individuals and groups in South Africa, who cannot accept the sharing of power; multinational corporations collude with and encourage this. The situation of African Americans did not really improve during the Presidency of an African American. On 2015's Selma to Montgomery 50th

Anniversary march there were two sets of placards. One read 'Black Lives Matter', witnessing to the spate of police shootings and the totally disproportionate number of black men and women in jails and on death row. The other read 'Restore Our Voting Rights', since many gains in the Martin Luther King era have been reversed to disenfranchise African Americans.

'What would Jesus do?' is a favourite question in some Christian circles. Jesus was the supreme breaker of barriers, meeting, befriending and affirming, as he did, Gentile soldiers of the occupying armies, women in an age when a 'good' religious Jew gave thanks that he was male, and folk with disabilities who were pitied or abandoned on a scrapheap. An African carried his cross, and a member of the Sanhedrin took his body from the rubbish dump for a decent burial. Yet if we look beyond the sanitised interpretation of the gospel, it is obvious that Jesus had to learn lessons and make a difficult journey to throw off the racial prejudice that divided Jews and Samaritans, to make the leap from calling a Samaritan woman who was drawing water at the well a 'dog' (a familiar insult), to making a compassionate Samaritan the hero of his most fundamental teaching about God and neighbour.

If he had to make that journey, we need to recognise, like Trevor Huddleston, that we all need to make it too. We need to listen to the stories and feel the pain of those who have suffered racism, not just proclaim our solidarity. So deeply ingrained is so much of our language that fosters a stereotype. Some of it hails from slavery in the British Empire. Few of us now would use the phrase that was common not so long ago, 'n----r in the woodpile', or describe a colour of shoe polish as 'n----r brown'. But do we realise that 'no skin off my back' relates to the torture of whipping, an everyday phenomenon in slavery times, and 'the nitty gritty' was the dirt left on the floor when incarcerated human beings were packed into slave ships. In Boston I learned to replace the term 'runaway slaves' with 'enslaved people who are self-liberated'. That's a good example of the dignity given to someone who has the courage to seek their full humanity, and we should always honour that. An attitude of respect and cultural affirmation assists us in reaching our potential in relationship with others. To go on to challenge the structural racism in our own and other societies is an act of solidarity, where in seeking full humanity for all, we begin to deepen and rediscover our own. Karen Armstrong, the writer on religion, claims that the authentic mark of any religion worth its name is compassion. It's often sneered at today, and seen as sentimental. In fact it was central to Jesus,

Muhammed, the Buddha, and every great religious leader. It is a tool to combat racism, individually and structurally.

Iain Whyte

God of hospitality

I saw a stranger yesterday.
I put food in the eating place,
Drink in the drinking place,
Music in the listening place
And, in the sacred name of the Triune God,
He blessed us and our house,
our cattle and our dear ones.
As the lark says in her song:
'Often, often, often,
goes the Christ in the stranger's guise.'

– Celtic Rune of Hospitality

God of hospitality,
we see strangers every day;
we hold back, we turn away;
fear is in us: fear controls us.
We have heard on the news and in idle gossip
that difference is dangerous,
different colours, different voices mean – what?
Maybe terrorism stalks our streets – Isis – Al-Qaida
might be lurking.
Shouts well up in us,
'Send them home!'
'They are not welcome.'

But, we forget.
To us, home means safety and food in the eating place.
To 'them' home might mean fear or poverty.
Or maybe their home is right here.

Maybe they have music in the listening place to share with us –
there are so many opportunities for strangers to become friends.

God of light and dark, shade and sunlight,
help us to recover our roots of friendship and hospitality.
Open us up: body, heart and soul
to the adventure of sharing the hospitality of others as we
reach out to them.
For we confess that we have often missed
the Christ in the stranger's guise
and impoverished the possibilities of new friendships
and new journeys in our lives.

Let us forget the fears that make us collude with racism and exclusion
and build together a more free and just society.
Amen

Isabel Whyte

Sources

1. *The Stephen Lawrence Inquiry Report of an Inquiry by Sir William Macpherson, 1999*

2. ibid.

Passages from NRSV copyright 1989, Division of Christian Education of the National Council of the Churches of Christ in the United States of America. Used by permission. All rights reserved.

Prayers for Remembrance Sunday

Roddy Cowie

Prayer for Remembrance Sunday (I)

God, our Father,
Christ, our brother,
Spirit, our inner life,
on this day we bring you our divided nature,
and we ask you to guide us.

Lord, we bring our shame.
We know your name is Prince of Peace.
We know that you said 'Thou shalt not kill.'
But human beings seem incapable of going for a decade
without a war.
Lord, we do not hide our shame.
We bring it openly to you:
Lord, hear us.
Lord, mercifully hear us.

Lord, we come before you in pride and thanks.
We remember people who have followed what they believed was right,
even when it meant the cost of their own lives.
Their sacrifice fills us with astonishment
and we give you thanks that such people exist.
Lord, we do not hide our pride and thanks.
We bring it openly to you:
Lord, hear us.
Lord, mercifully hear us.

Lord, we bring you our confusion,
and we ask you to resolve the chaos in our disordered souls.
Without you we are helpless in the storm of our divided nature.
Speak, Lord, calm the storm,
and lead us back to the harbour of your peace.
Lord, we do not hide our confusion.
We bring it openly to you:
Lord, hear us.
Lord, mercifully hear us.

Lord, we bring you our hope.
May we put our trust in the power of good to overcome evil,
the power of love to overcome hatred.
We pray to you for the power to be gentle,
the strength to be forgiving,
the patience to be understanding
and the endurance to accept the consequences
of holding to what we believe is right.

Help us to devote our thought and energy,
our whole life,
to the task of making peace,
praying always for the inspiration and power to fulfil this destiny
for which all people were created.
Lord, we do not hide our hope.
We bring it openly to you:
Lord, hear us.
Lord, mercifully hear us.

Prayer for Remembrance Sunday (II)

Jesus, Prince of Peace,
today we look back on a century scarred with war,
and ask you to guide our remembrance.

We bring you our remembrance of the two World Wars,
confused and bewildering as it is.
We bring you our childhood memories of heroic soldiers –
brothers and uncles, fathers and grandfathers –
and our memories of families grieving for loved ones.
We bring you our gratitude for self-sacrifice
and our sadness at loss,
our despair that wars like that could ever happen,
and our inability to understand it all.
We bring you, too, all we have learned since
about the heroism of people we had only thought of as enemies,
and the destruction done by our own side,
and other families grieving.

Jesus, we bring you our remembrances.
Help us to understand the truth
and shape the future.

We bring you our cloudy remembrances of wars
that we noticed for a while and then forgot,
because the countries were a long way off,
wars in *(name countries …)*.
We know our sympathy for our fellow human beings tends to fade
with the images on the TV screen,
and yet their pain goes on.

Jesus, we bring you our remembrances.
Help us to understand the truth
and shape the future.

We bring you our remembrances of wars in our own country,
Christian against Christian, divided by heartfelt loyalties
and points of doctrine.

Jesus, forgive us for the harm we have done
to the name of Christianity and for our inability to see
how Christian love should have been lived out
here on our own soil.

Jesus, we bring you our remembrances.
**Help us to understand the truth
and shape the future.**

We pray especially for the victims of war –
the disabled, those scarred mentally,
the bereaved, the indoctrinated, the embittered …
for cities laid waste, countries impoverished, generations uneducated.
Uphold them with your power to bring healing and forgiveness,
and instruct your servants what to do;
help us to remember that what we do to them,
or fail to do, we do to you.

Jesus, we bring you our remembrances.
**Help us to understand the truth
and shape the future.**

Prayer for Remembrance Sunday (III)

Lord God, we come before you
and look back over the long years.
We see the endless foolishness of humanity,
drawn towards war like shards of iron to a magnet.
Lord, have mercy.
Christ, have mercy.

Lord God, we come before you
and look back over the long years.
We see the young lives that war has ended, and lives left blighted –
those physically disabled,
those widowed or orphaned,
the shattered communities.
We see the minds left broken by fear or bitterness.
The soldiers coming back to a world that seems to have no place for them,
and little real understanding of the price they paid.
We pray for all the victims of the wars of the last long century.
Lord, have mercy.
Christ, have mercy.

Lord God, we come before you,
and we see the present.
The horrors of the wars in the Middle East.
The dangerous tensions between great powers.
The grinding conflicts that we barely hear of in so many countries.
The blight of terrorism suddenly striking innocent people anywhere.
We pray for those who suffer war, and those who work for peace.

Lord God, we lift our eyes to powers and governments
facing a world full of uncertainty,
searching for ways to move into the future.
We pray for the leaders of great powers
whose choices shape the future of our world.
We pray for our Prime Minister and for the leaders of our country.
Remind all leaders how little pride and profit count
beside the blessing of peace.

And how little loss of prestige or arguments counts
beside the loss of life.
Lord, have mercy.
Christ, have mercy.

On this Remembrance Sunday, we give special thanks
for those who have stood in the firing line
and put others' lives before their own.
We pray for those who make the same commitment now.
Shield them from danger, and from the temptations of their calling.
Lord, have mercy.
Christ, have mercy.

In all this, Lord, we pray for your church.
May its voice speak for peace
and show the way to justice and equality.
Speak through your bishops, priests, ministers
and the ordinary people of your church.
Help us to aid each other in the work
of bringing light and peace into a stormy world.
Lord, have mercy.
Christ, have mercy.

Finally, Lord, we bring before you those who are close to us.
Those we love, and those who love us;
those we work with, and those who work with us;
those we have difficulty with, and those who have difficulty with us.
All these people we bring before you in the silence,
and we pray for health to strengthen them
and your light to guide them towards you.
Lord, have mercy.
Christ, have mercy.

The light which illumines the world

Readings, reflections and prayers for the four weeks of Advent

Peter Millar

Introduction:

Advent is a time of both celebration and reflection. It is a time of waiting and of expectancy. In the following thoughts I hold together these traditional themes. The Bible and our daily living are always intertwined. The Creator's light and hope resonate at the heart of the universe and in the depths of our being. Each day in the Iona Community we share words which express this amazing truth both poetically and succinctly. They are words for all seasons, including Advent:

In work and worship,
God is with us.

Gathered and scattered,
God is with us.

Now and always,
God is with us.

From the Iona Community's daily 'office'

The first week of Advent: The promise of liberation

Scripture sentences:

… Stand upright and hold your heads high, because your liberation is near.
Luke 21:28

Awake, sleeper, rise from the dead, and Christ will shine upon you.
Ephesians 5:14

The watchmen raise their voices and shout together in joy, for with their own eyes they see the Lord return to Zion.
Isaiah 52:8

Bible readings:

Jeremiah 33:14–16; Psalm 25:1–10; 1 Thessalonians 3:9–13; Luke 21:25–36

Reflection:

The possibility that we can experience liberation in body, mind and spirit is a central theme in Christianity. It is also a core teaching in many of the world's other great religions. The liberation of peoples is also a dominant issue in our divided modern world. In this first week of Advent the gospel tells us that we can stand upright and hold our heads high, because our liberation is near.

Some religions teach us that liberation, the freeing of the soul, implies a major move away from the sordidness and pain of the world, into a place of release, of quietude, often distant from worldly concerns. This emphasis is also present in some expressions of contemporary Christianity. In this interpretation the world is considered a totally sinful place from which Christ frees us. In my understanding, liberation in Jesus is much more about finding a place of inner hope and healing within the contradictions and questions of daily living. Over the years the Iona Community has been committed to holding a vision in which our Christian convictions are always intertwined with everyday happenings. Therefore the message of Advent directly connects to the pluralities and surprises of society. Certainly we can hold our heads high because liberation is at hand, but always in the midst of the marketplace. As the Lord comes, he comes again and again in the midst of his people as they are, warts and all. It is no different this year!

Yet especially in our time we must use the word liberation with sensitivity. Millions of our sisters and brothers long for liberation from oppressive rulers and have not found it. Instead they have found war and its terrible aftermath. Their initially peaceful marches for liberation have brought unremitting violence. We all know the story.

Yet is it not because of our faith in Christ which brings us this inner freedom that we are propelled to be in loving solidarity with all those who are not free, either in body or in spirit? Abraham Heschel put that truth this way:

'God created a reminder, an image.
Humanity is a reminder of God.
As God is compassionate, let humanity be compassionate.' [1]

Advent calls us again to consider and to experience *'Christ's shining'*. You may find that difficult if you are depressed or feeling abandoned. Sit quietly and read the Bible passages suggested. Try to see your life in a wider frame of meaning. I know that I have to do that often these days, having lived for almost three years with an incurable cancer inside me. It is easy to be downcast, yet let us remember that God's purposes are forever at work in ourselves, even in the darkest night.

Prayer:

Thank you, Lord, in this first week of Advent
for breaking again into our world in all of its hopes and pains
and complexities.
We are grateful for every sign of your liberating love
within that world and in ourselves.

The second week of Advent: Changing direction

Scripture sentences:

The Lord God has warned them time and again through his messengers, for he took pity on his people and on his dwelling place.

2 Chronicles 36:15

They will know that they have a prophet among them, whether they listen or whether in their rebelliousness they refuse to listen.

Ezekiel 2:5

The Prophet of the Most High will be the Lord's forerunner, to prepare his way and lead his people to a knowledge of salvation through the forgiveness of their sins.

Luke 1:76–77

Bible readings:

Malachi 3:1–14; Psalm 27; Philippians 1:3–11; Luke 3:7–18

Reflection:

In this second week of Advent we are being invited to look again at the priorities in our lives and to experience anew the wide-ranging forgiveness of God. It is also a time within the Christian year to reflect on what it means to say that we allow the Holy Spirit to direct and inform our daily actions. The prophet Ezekiel reminds us that purposeful listening to God's guidance is a free choice. We can walk away from it, or we can take it to heart.

In an age in which most of us are bewildered by all the choices possible, this core choice remains with us each day in the form of a tender invitation from the One who longs for us to be awakened in our depths and to share in the light which illumines the world. To experience what I would call 'that quiet knowledge' which makes us, as the theologian Hans Küng would say, *'fully human'*.

In *The Rule of Benedict* we read that everything we think, everything we do, everything we feel is irreplaceable and thus makes each moment hallowed. And this relates us to the understanding of the sacredness of humanity. God above us, beside us, beneath us: our beginning and our end.

When we think about God calling us back to where we truly belong, we soon encounter various paradoxes. And some of these link directly to the way in which society is structured. For a start, we are all restless. No one would argue with the fact that society is not always at ease with itself, and our own lives in one way or another mirror this turbulence. That is not to suggest that we don't seek an inner cohesion, but for a huge percentage of us life is a twisting path.

Yet in the face of our many inner and outer contradictions, it may be that the importance of the Advent message lies in the utter simplicity of this basic invitation to take stock and look into ourselves. In these weeks before Christmas we are given an opportunity to become aware of healings of a deeper kind. Even with all the incredible technology which encompasses our lives, we still need space to reach into who we actually are: precious people created in the image of God. From time to time, we still need to ask of ourselves what is going on day by day with our emotions, with our feelings, with our inner lives. All of us have fears, inner contradictions and longings. Are we able to discard our illusions which cleverly mask much of who we really are and experience these God-given moments of creative vulnerability?

Given the pace of modern living it is easy to live rather blandly and to forget our great heritage of faith, of the spiritual search and of biblical truth. In the 6th century, living with just basic needs, Celtic monks spent years copying the Psalms and surrounding the words with artwork which even today takes the breath away. Let your imagination sit alongside one of these monks as these words appear on his page: *'I have asked of the Lord for one thing; one thing only do I want: to live in the Lord's house all my life, to marvel there at his goodness, and to ask for his guidance'* (Ps 27:4). And as you imagine the scene, allow your own mind to be penetrated by the truth within the words. To be changed by them. To risk being surprised by them! To be able to echo the old hymn which says: *'O speak to reassure me, to hasten or control; O speak, and make me listen, Thou guardian of my soul ...'*

Prayer:

Lord, there are many parts in me
which need to change direction.
Not tomorrow, but today.
In stillness help me to listen to the Lord's voice
and to realise that new transforming journeys lie ahead,
pathways rich in surprise,
blessing and truth.

The third week of Advent: Watching and waiting

Scripture sentences:

I wait for the Lord with longing; I put my hope in his word. My soul waits for the Lord more eagerly than watchmen for the morning.

Psalm 130:5–6

The Lord is good to those who look to him, to anyone who seeks him; it is good to wait in patience for deliverance by the Lord.

Lamentations 3:25–26

I shall stand at my post; I shall take up my position on the watchtower, keeping a lookout to learn what the Lord says to me.

Habakkuk 2:1

Bible readings:

Zephaniah 3:14–20; Psalm 45; Philippians 4:4–7; Luke 3:7–18

Reflection:

As we think about watching and waiting in Advent, these prophetic words from *A Wee Worship Book* can help us to place so much in perspective:

For all that God can do within us,
for all that God can do without us,
thanks be to God.

For all in whom Christ lives before us,
for all in whom Christ lives beside us,
thanks be to God.

For all the Spirit wants to bring us,
for where the Spirit wants to send us,
thanks be to God.[2]

These beautiful and comforting words invite us to deepest meaning of waiting and of watching. They throw open the great canvas of our lives, of our world and of God's presence within it all. This is not a description of a small God who is at hand to fulfil our every wish. Quite the opposite. In the 4th century, Gregory of Nyssa, writing about the creation of humankind, said this: *'It is the whole of nature, extending from the beginning to the end that constitutes the one image of God who is.'*[3] My friend, the late Bede Griffiths of South India, talked often about the *'cosmic Christ'* – the One in whom everything ultimately comes together. A truth I was expressing when I wrote this prayer some years ago when living in Australia:

God of bush and bog-myrtle, of old man banksia and dancing birch, of sheltering aspen and huon pine, of heather and eucalypt, illumine our minds that we may embrace your sacred earth with renewed tenderness and rejoice in a cosmos imbued with your wisdom.

It's so important that in Advent we are not waiting on a God of our own making: just a larger version of ourselves! With many others on the pilgrim path, I think it would enlarge the vision of thousands of people if in these Advent days our churches and temples were not filled just with prayers and thoughts about ourselves, our families, our near neighbours – important as they all are in the eyes of God – but also about the wider world in which we hear the tears of millions; about the wounding and breaking of creation; about our endless enslavements to power, greed and money; about the generations yet unborn. Thus allowing us to enter more meaningfully into the mystery of God. Giving us an opportunity to recognise that Native Americans are right when they tell us that we are relatives of all that live upon our gentle, welcoming earth. To hear again all those who remind us that the weak ones in our society have so much to teach us.

Prayer:

Lord of Advent,
come to our world of military might, political blindness and fake news,
and overturn our tired ideas of power and glory
until your wisdom invades our understanding.

The fourth week of Advent: The awakening

Scripture sentences:

A virgin will conceive and bear a son, and he shall be called Emmanuel – a name which means 'God is with us'.

Matthew 1:23

My soul tells out the greatness of the Lord, my spirit has rejoiced in God my Saviour.

Luke 1:46–47

Rejoice, daughter of Zion! I am coming; I shall make my dwelling among you, says the Lord.

Zechariah 2:10

Bible readings:

Micah 5:2–5; Psalm 80:1–7; Hebrews 10:5–10; Luke 1:3–45

Reflection:

On the day before his death, the ninety-six-year-old Zen Buddhist sage D.T. Suzuki wrote that we should *'aspire so to live that along with Meister Eckhart we can say that "Christ is born every moment in my soul"'*.[4]

And people like Suzuki all encourage us, in this time of festivity, to think about the world in all of its incredible and myriad variety. In affluent nations many are shopping as if there was no tomorrow. Yet even in places of great prosperity folk are sleeping on the streets. In war-torn countries millions will be spending Christmas amidst the ruins of their homes. In the vast slum areas which surround hundreds of great cities, millions of families will be trying to make it a good Christmas for their families despite gut-wrenching poverty. In other places, Christmas morning will mean the birth of a child or the death of a loved one. Bells will ring out and candles will be lit to remind us again of that birth in Bethlehem all those years ago. As Prudentius, the 4th century hymn writer, puts it: *'Of the Father's love begotten, ere the world's began to be, He is Alpha and Omega; He the source, the ending He, of the things that are, that have been, and that future years shall see ...'*

In the midst of it all, our restless, searching hearts and minds can actually be opened, moment by moment, to the illumination (the shining) of God in Christ. In other words, that we are able to move beyond our own limited comprehension of what life is about, into an entirely different perspective of meaning and of purpose. It was reading *The Rule of Benedict* which first taught me more about this. Through reading the Rule I came to see that the Christian faith is a constant movement of awakening and reawakening to God's presence at the core of our being. This journey within humanity begins in the timeless ages, but it comes to a particular outpouring in the events of the first Christmas. There is an old Indian saying which goes like this: *'God has lit up some lamps in my heart that nothing can put out.'*

And as we touch into these inner lamps in Advent we are also called to a renewed discipleship: invited to be witnesses for Jesus in the world. And if we find it difficult to understand the word 'witness' in our plural world, we may find some words of the late Cardinal John Henry Newman to be helpful. Newman died many years ago. As a church leader his life of compassion touched people in a special way. In our time when we try to make what we say and write politically correct his language may appear old fashioned, yet his words still hold their power and wisdom:

'God has created me to do Him some definite service. He has committed some work to me which He has not committed to another. I have my mission ... I am a link in the chain, a bond of connection between persons. He has not created me for naught. I shall do good; I shall do his work. I shall be ... a preacher of truth in my own place, while not intending it if I do but keep His commandments. Therefore, I will trust Him, whatever I am, I can never be thrown away ... He does nothing in vain. The Lord knows what He is about.' [5]

With these tender yet challenging words in our minds, let us together be ready to welcome Christ this Christmas. To believe the words of the poster: *'God so loved this world that she/he got involved.'* To stand in solidarity with all who are in need, and with pilgrims everywhere say together: *'We affirm God's goodness at the heart of humanity, planted more deeply than all that is wrong.'* [6]

Prayer:

Lord, kindle in our hearts within
a flame of love to our neighbours,
to our foes, to our friends, to our loved ones all,
from the lowliest thing that lives,
to the name that is highest of all.

Gaelic traditional

Sources and acknowledgements:

1. Abraham Heschel, 'Abraham Joshua Heschel's Last Words: An Interview by Carl Stern', *Intellectual Digest,* June 1972, p.78

2. From *A Wee Worship Book (5th Incarnation)*, Wild Goose Resource Group, copyright © 2016 WGRG, c/o Iona Community, Glasgow, Scotland. www.wildgoose.scot

3. Gregory of Nyssa, source of translation unknown

4. From Donald Nicholl

5. 'Mission of my life', John Henry Newman

6. From an Iona Community affirmation, *Iona Abbey Worship Book*, 2017 © Iona Community

Voices of longing, glimpses of hope
A script for six voices for the beginning of an Advent service
Elaine Gisbourne

Church in darkness, 'stage' empty, except for a crib positioned front centre (we used an orange box with a piece of hessian sacking for bedding).

Voice 1: Prophet, holding a large lit candle, positioned back centre stage

Voice 2: Elderly person, bereaved, living alone

Voice 3: Young mum/dad living on benefits

Voice 4: Homeless young person sleeping rough

Voice 5: Refugee, asylum seeker

Voice 6: Mary, holding an unlit tea-light, offstage at start

Voices 2, 3, 4, 5 can be positioned two stage left, two stage right, behind crib, or around the body of the church – however your space lends itself.

Music: 'Let all mortal flesh keep silence' (sung solo and unaccompanied from the back of the church, first verse only)

Raise lights sufficiently to allow actors to be seen and to be able to read their scripts.

Voice 1: The people walk in darkness …

Voice 2: After all our years together, I can't get used to being on my own. We were 17 when we met, and in 64 years of marriage we never spent a night apart, and now I'm so lonely. It's the long, dark nights that are the worst; and I can go for days without speaking to anyone. I remember when our house was full of noise and chatter and mess – now I long for a mess to tidy up!

Voice 1: The people walk in darkness …

Voice 3: It's exhausting, just trying to get through each day. There's not enough of anything: not enough work, not enough money, not enough food, not enough warmth, not enough sleep. When I look

Voices of longing, glimpses of hope   207

at the kids I just think about what a bad *mum/dad* I am – I can't give them what they need.

Voice 1:   The people walk in darkness …

Voice 4:   My social worker got me into a hostel, but I could only stay if I stayed off the drink. It was going OK, but two days ago I heard my dad died and I couldn't handle it. I got drunk and got kicked out.

Voice 1:   The people walk in darkness …

Voice 5:   When our home was bombed, we had nowhere to go, we had nothing. We got to the camp, and it was a relief. There was shelter and food, and over time the children were able to sleep again; their nightmares were less frequent. But there was no school for them, and no work for us, and no sign that we would ever be able to rebuild our lives again. No sign that the war would end and we would be able to go home.

Voice 1:   To the people who walk in darkness, a light will come …

Voice 6:   *(moves forward and lights her candle from the one held by the prophet; moves centre stage)* When the angel spoke, he set my heart on fire – I have never known such joy! To think that God knows me, and chose me, that He trusts me to do this for Him, for the world! I said 'Yes' to God. I said 'Yes' to the possibility that the world might be a different place, and that I might have a part to play in that coming true!

Voice 1:   A light will come …

Voice 2:   I get scared when I think that no one would know if I was unwell; if I had a fall, I could be on the floor for days. Who would care?

Voice 1:   A light will come …

Voice 3:   You can't give up – you have to keep trying, for the kids. You have to swallow your pride, keep applying for jobs that never give you a second look, just to get the benefits and the voucher for the food bank.

Voice 1: A light will come …

Voice 4: At night the cold freezes me, literally, my bones, my blood. I'm stiff, I hurt everywhere. If I can get a drink, it's only the booze that keeps me warm. I don't know what's worse: the people who kick me and swear at me, or the ones who walk by and ignore me like I'm invisible. Time is about the only thing I have plenty of. I spend hours and hours wishing my life was different.

Voice 1: A light will come …

Voice 5: We had to give all our money to the men with the boat: it was our only hope, our only way to safety. The journey was terrifying, but what can you do? If we'd stayed we would have had no life anyway. We have to take our chances and hope we can be safe somewhere.

Voice 1: A light for the path …

Voice 6: But now I am afraid, far from home, only Joseph and strangers around me. I am so heavy, so tired, and this journey – will it never end?

Voice 1: A light to shine in the darkness …

Voice 6: And who will help me, when my time comes?

Voice 2: And who will help me?

Voice 3: Who will help us?

Voice 4: Who will help, who can I trust?

Voice 5: And where will we be welcome?

Voice 1: A light for all people …

Voice 6: The child stirs and turns in me, and when I rub my belly he moves with me. Sometimes he jumps and jerks, like hiccups. When I sing to him he stills to my voice.

Voice 1: The night will shine as the day …

Voice 6: When I'm afraid, I remember how I felt when the angel came; the memory of his words calms me. That's the voice I must listen to.

Voice 1: And all the people will see the light …

Voice 6: He kicks so hard now, and pushes at me, as though he can't wait to be born. But the road still stretches ahead; we are not safe here, and it is not his time yet. Your time is close, little one, but please, not yet.

Voice 1: All people will walk in the light …

Voice 6: Soon, but not yet, little one, not yet. *(Sets candle down at head of the crib.)*

All actors remain in position while a solo, unaccompanied voice from the back of the church sings 'Come down, O love divine' (first verse).

Then all characters move off.

The lights come up in the church.

The appointment
A reflection on the Incarnation

Tom Gordon

You kept your appointment,
just like you said you would.
You promised,
and I believed you.
Well, that's what faith's about, isn't it?
You didn't say when or how you would come.
But you said you would.

You assured me it was true,
that you would keep your word.
And you did.
You kept your appointment.
And because I didn't know when or how,
I almost missed it.

You didn't come running down a station platform
with your arms thrown out wide,
and me the welcoming party of one.
You didn't come in a cavalcade,
with ticker-tape falling,
and a band playing,
and me waving a flag
with lots of others.

I almost missed it.

Well, it was so unexpected,
the manger,
and the stable,
and the baby,
and all the rest.
But you came.

You kept your appointment,
just like you said you would.
You promised,
and I believed you.
Well, that's what faith's about, isn't it?

You didn't say when or how you would come.
But you said you would.

You assured me it was true,
that you would keep your word.
And you did.
You kept your appointment.
And because I didn't know when or how,
I almost missed it.

When I struggled with living,
and loving,
and learning,
you came.
You didn't come in a blinding revelation,
with angel voices,
and a fanfare of trumpets,
and me leaping up and down.

I almost missed it.

Well, it was so unexpected,
the feeling of reassurance
in a kindly word,
a tender touch,
a sense of wonder,
and much more besides.
But you came.

You kept your appointment,
just like you said you would.
You promised,
and I believed you.
Well, that's what faith's about, isn't it?

The Gospel according to sheep

An alternative look at Christmas

Janet Lees

This was first performed at a school in Yorkshire, which is a very sheepy place.

For it you will need:

– A chorus of sheep
– A professor, or professors (male and female)
– Readers
– The (female) voice of God (could be someone unseen using a mic)
– John

Songs, carols, music, silence, a dance for sheep, artwork, etc can all be added anywhere throughout.

Professor: When God first got the idea of sheep it was just one small idea in a much bigger idea called 'the universe'. Indeed, this Big Idea was so big it has taken billions of human lifetimes to get as far as we have today in understanding it – and we're still quite a long way from really getting God's Big Idea.

Along the way, some human beings remembered stories of God's ideas and wrote them down in what is now the Bible. This is not all the good ideas God ever had, just some of the ones that have been remembered and written down. But amongst those ideas are things about sheep. Sheep may not seem that great to some of you, but the fact is, God rates sheep and included them in the Big Idea. Human beings, and sheep too, have remembered that. In the Bible there are lots of stories about sheep. And we're going to tell you some today.

Song or carol: 'While shepherds watched', or another sheepy song or carol

Professor: The Big Idea didn't begin with sheep. It began with space and time, and light and dark, and a thing called the firmament.

All sheep: What's that?

Professor: The firmament is the sky above us and the earth beneath us – together they make up the firmament. Without the firmament there would be no place for sheep and humans to live.

Bible reading: Genesis 1:1–5 (We used an easy-to-read version.)

A sheep: What about the sheep?

Professor: Well, sheep didn't appear straight away. It took God a couple of days to get round to them, and all the other animals, including people.

God: *(female voice please)* Now, let me see. Let the water be filled with many kinds of living creatures, and the air be filled with birds. Let the earth produce all kinds of animals, tame and wild, large and small …

Professor: And God saw all that and was very pleased. Time went by. Sheep and people lived side by side. But people were not as reliable as God would have liked them to be. People kept misbehaving, doing bad things to each other and spoiling the world. Eventually, God had had enough of this.

A sheep: What about us sheep? What were we doing all this time?

Professor: That's a good question. The Bible doesn't mention this, but I think the sheep were just getting on with being sheep, living in flocks and eating and growing, having lambs and so on.

All sheep: Sounds good.

Professor: So, as I was saying, God had enough of people's bad behaviour, and so, reluctantly, God decided to destroy the earth with a flood. But before that happened, God noticed Noah.

God: Noah, I want you to build an ark. It needs to be big and strong. I am going to send a flood to destroy the world and I want you and your family to take enough animals into the ark so that after the flood the world can begin again.

Professor: So Noah started building the ark. He got quite a lot of teasing and comments from his neighbours. But he just got on with the job God had given him to do. Eventually, the ark was finished and Noah and his family started to put the animals inside. The animals went in two by two.

All sheep: What about us?

Professor: Don't worry, two sheep went into the ark with all the other animals. The rain came and the earth was flooded, and for 40 days and nights the ark floated on the floodwater before coming to rest on a mountain. After that, all the animals came out (probably more than went in). Then God sent a sign to Noah and his family that this would never happen again.

Bible reading: Genesis 9:8–17

A sheep: What happened next? Are there more stories about sheep?

Professor: Yes, there are lots, but we haven't got time for them all. Perhaps we could just have the most important ones.

All sheep: Yes, the most important ones.

Professor: But maybe first, now would be a good time for a song about sheep, to celebrate how important they are in God's world.

All sheep: Yes please: a song about sheep.

Professor: People have made up lots of songs to sing to God. One of them in the Bible is called 'The Lord is my Shepherd'.

Song: 'The Lord is my shepherd' (any version folk know)

A sheep: I'm getting tired now. I need to go to sleep. Have you got a nice story to send us to sleep please?

Professor: I'll do my best. How about the best story of all?

All sheep: Yes, the best story of all.

Professor: Settle down then, and listen carefully … Two thousand years ago some sheep were witnesses to a very special event. It was the night that God's son was born, and this is what happened.

(You might want carols, like 'O, little town of Bethlehem', between each of the following readings, or instrumental music, or silence instead.)

Bible readings: Luke 2:1–7; Luke 2:8–14; Luke 2:15–20

All sheep: That was lovely.

A sheep: So is that it now? Are there any more stories in the Bible about sheep?

Professor: There are lots and lots.

A sheep: So can we have another one please?

Professor: All right, but this really must be the last one … When Jesus grew up into an adult, he started to travel around Galilee with a group of friends, telling stories and healing people. The stories were a good way of explaining to people God's plan for the world and God's special relationship with human beings.

All sheep: And sheep!

Professor: Yes, of course, and with sheep. Take this story about 100 sheep.

All sheep: How many?

A sheep: Did you say 100 sheep?

Professor: That's right. A shepherd was looking after a large flock of 100 sheep. Each night he would lead them to the sheepfold and they would sleep safely for the night. He would watch over them, and each night he would count them just to make sure every sheep was safely inside.

All sheep: Safe and sound.

Professor: But what would happen if one sheep got lost? What would the shepherd do then, do you think?

Bible reading: Luke 15:4–7

Professor: You may be wondering how the story of God's Big Idea ends. Well, in some ways it never ends because we keep telling the story to each other, and so the story goes on and on. But there is a story at the end of the Bible about a man called John, who lived on an island in the Mediterranean Sea, who had a dream.

John: *(waking up)* I've just had a dream about heaven and what it will be like there.

All sheep: What will it be like?

John: There will be a golden city with a river running down the middle of the street and trees growing there with special healing fruits.

All sheep: Sounds lovely.

John: God will be there to welcome us all home, and no one will ever be upset or sad about things ever again. There will be no need to cry.

All sheep: Sounds happy.

John: And Jesus will be there on a special throne, and he will be like a lamb. You see, sheep are important to God.

All sheep: We know.

Professor: Yes, we know that sheep are important to God. And if sheep are important to God, how much more valued by God are we human beings. So important in fact that God sent Jesus to be born like one of us and live alongside us and be with us forever. This is what we celebrate at Christmas. It's the gospel, the good news about Jesus, God's own son.

All sheep: And sheep!

Carol: 'Hark the herald angels sing'

The council of the Magi
A dialogue

Richard Skinner

This piece could be acted out or read.

Enter Balthazar, suitably dressed for a wise and mighty eastern potentate. He addresses the audience.

Balthazar: Greetings! You are all very welcome. My name is Balthazar, and I am the ruler of a country in the eastern part of the world. As well as being the ruler, I am also known as a 'magus', which means 'wise man'. I am not boasting when I say that; it simply means that over the years I have devoted myself to study and learning. In particular, I have made a lifetime study of the sky, of the movements of the stars and the planets and the strange phenomena that can sometimes be seen there. One of the main beliefs of my people and myself is that what takes place in the sky can tell us much about what is taking place, or will take place, here on earth, provided we interpret the signs correctly. For me to be a good ruler of my people, it is therefore important that I and my advisers study the stars and all that happens in the heavens so that we may know what the future holds, to be forewarned of times of famine or flood, or the attack of enemies; and also to know the favourable times for undertaking new projects: the planting of crops, the building of dams and temples.

Several months ago, something really strange started to occur in the sky. A new star appeared. Quite dim at first, but over the following days and weeks this star has grown ever brighter – until now it is so bright that everyone can see it even during the daytime.

The appearance of this new, bright star is of utmost importance, for it indicates that some event of tremendous significance is about to occur somewhere on the earth. I have of course consulted all my books of wisdom to try to interpret correctly what this significant event will be and where it will take place – or will it be worldwide? I have managed to calculate much, but remain puzzled about many aspects of the event; and so, working on the belief that two heads are better than one, and three heads are better than two, I have sent messengers to the rulers of the two countries which border my own, suggesting that the three of us meet to exchange ideas and together work out the full meaning of this new star. I am happy to say that both of them, wise men like myself, have agreed to my suggestion and have just arrived for the meeting. Their names are Melchior and Caspar, and we are about to begin our discussion. You are welcome to listen.

Balthazar turns and welcomes Melchior and Caspar who enter, dressed similar to Balthazar. The three men sit together.

Balthazar: My brothers in wisdom, I thank you for coming here to discuss what could well be the approach of a momentous event. Brother Melchior, what understanding have you arrived at concerning this strange new star?

Melchior: Brother Balthazar, brother Caspar, I have studied very closely many aspects of the star: the exact time and date when it first appeared in the sky, the manner in which it has grown in brightness, its actual position compared with the other fixed stars, its relationship with the wandering planets. My interpretation of all these factors and others is that it is a sign that a very important birth will take place in a few months' time. Not here, in one of our three countries, but hundreds of miles to the west. The birth will be of a future king. Not, as far as I can determine, the king of one particular country, but as king or ruler of all countries. A mighty king, a wise ruler. Mightier and wiser, I may say, than I could ever hope to be! The expression that my studies have led me to is that of 'King of kings'.

Balthazar: Thank you, brother Melchior. Brother Caspar, what conclusions have your studies brought you to?

Caspar: I certainly agree with our brother Melchior that the star we can see is announcing a birth. My books of knowledge however lead me to the conclusion that the baby soon to be born has been specially chosen by God to reveal to the world more of God than has previously been revealed. In fact, the way I interpret the signs, the baby will grow up into a man so open to the will of God that everything he says and does will be exactly as though

God himself were saying it and doing it. He will be so filled with the love of God and the wisdom of God and the knowledge of God that we will be able to say, 'If you want to know what God is like, this man's life says it all.' That is my understanding of what the new star portends.

Balthazar: Brother Caspar, we thank you. Your studies clearly complement those of brother Melchior.

Melchior: And what of your own studies, brother Balthazar? Do you concur, or have you reached different conclusions?

Balthazar: Indeed. I most certainly agree with you both that the star foretells a birth, a birth of unparalleled significance. But as I have studied my texts, a sense of grave foreboding has emerged. The signs also tell of suffering and death ahead. Although the life of the child about to be born will be of overwhelming importance, so too will be his death and what follows. I perceive it will herald a new era for the world. However, my books of wisdom have not enabled me to interpret it more clearly than that – it is, I confess, almost as though their usefulness is coming to an end.

Caspar: I agree. The current dispensation has almost run its course. If my books could talk, they would be falling silent.

Melchior: Exactly so. Our wisdom, my brothers, though great, is being superseded by a far greater Wisdom.

Balthazar: Let us sum up. We're agreed that a birth is about to take place of one who will become a mighty and wise ruler, the 'King of kings'; whose life will speak to us of the mysteries of God; who will experience suffering, and whose death will usher in a new era.

Melchior and Caspar nod in agreement.

Caspar: In the light of these conclusions, should we not decide how to respond?

Melchior: What is our wisest course of action?

Caspar: We must visit. We must go and pay homage, and give thanks for his birth.

Melchior: And we must take gifts, gifts to show our understanding of who he is and why his birth is so significant.

Balthazar: What gifts would you suggest, Melchior?

Melchior: I will take gold, the royal metal. It is both precious and beautiful, which is why our crowns are made from gold. By bringing the gift of gold to the baby, we will be announcing, 'We recognise that you will be a king, a mighty king.'

Caspar: And I will take frankincense. It is of course the aromatic incense we add to our lamps and candles when we are praying, and we like to suppose that the sweet-smelling smoke it produces carries our prayers to heaven. The gift of frankincense to the baby will be our way of acknowledging that we recognise God's presence in him.

Balthazar: Very good. And I will take myrrh, the perfume we use when people have died and are about to be buried. We put myrrh on their bodies as a way of honouring them and showing that we mourn them, so in giving myrrh to the baby we will be both honouring him and preparing him for the suffering and death that lies ahead.

Caspar: If this birth is so important, as we clearly agree, surely we need also to discuss what difference we believe it will make to the way things are. What are our hopes about it? And indeed our fears?

Melchior: I would very much hope that as a mighty and wise king, he will be able to bring justice and peace to this world of ours. Too often there are wars and rumours of wars, and it is the duty of a ruler to guide and protect his people. I will admit though that, on a more selfish level, it concerns me that I might get deposed and no longer be a king. So the question does arise that if he is going to be a mighty king over all, what will happen to me? And what is going to happen to you two as well? That is my anxiety. And you, brother Caspar?

Caspar: My main hope is that because his life will show us what God is like, everyone will learn more of God because of him, and how to live the life God intends for us. On the other hand, my main fear is that God's ideas will be so different from my ideas that frankly I won't be able to understand them. And as I enjoy being thought wise, that's a rather disturbing prospect.

Balthazar: And as for me, my brothers, my hope is that the suffering and death I see in store for the child will somehow shed light on the suffering and death that blights all our lives. That is a problem that none of us has ever been able to solve, and our books of knowledge are of no help. My fear, therefore, is that his suffering and death will fail to clarify these mysteries, and indeed might show us that there is no answer possible, and so all will have been in vain. That is my fear.

Melchior: But only the future will reveal which of our hopes and which of our fears come to pass.

Balthazar: My brothers, we have spoken together enough. It is now time for action. If we are to make our visit, we must make good speed and leave soon. Let us go and prepare for the journey.

The three men rise, bow formally to each other, then to the audience, and process out.

In shop doorways and on street corners

A reflection, meditation, and ideas for taking action on homelessness

Ewan Aitken

In shop doorways and on street corners: a reflection

I heard these stories one night when I was out with the Cyrenians street team. Each story is different yet holds in common the cry of human fragility and struggle, of broken bodies and ground-down souls, often by the system which is supposed to help.

Take Mo and Tam: grappling with addiction, they once had a house. This had been through a move from temporary to permanent accommodation – which should have been the first step to a new life, but because it also involved a move to Universal Credit, about which they were given very little guidance or support, rent arrears accrued. And so the system said eviction. Not 'how did you get into this situation and what can we do to help?' They sought help from family in another city, but it was refused. They presented themselves as homeless in their new city, but because they have no local connection have to wait up to six months to be eligible for help. Six months sleeping rough: because the system gatekeeps first and asks questions later. Home now is a tent in a graveyard …

Sean was outside a supermarket. He had a place in a B&B but said the staff there looked down on him and were patronising and rude. Staying there was more damaging to his soul than sleeping in a doorway …

Bobby has been bouncing around the streets and hostels for nine years. He was in a doorway asking for food. He said he was on methadone. He wanted to come off it but his partner didn't, and it was her house he was in now. His choice seemed to be between coming off drugs, but losing his relationship and home, and staying on drugs to ensure he had a place to stay and a partner …

Alex was lying in his own sick outside a pub. I thought he'd been begging at first. My colleague and I worked out that he had a place in a hostel nearby but was ill. Not drunk, but ill. That, combined with his disability, meant he couldn't make it back to the hostel – so we got him there. The staff took him in with kind words and compassion. He's been there a long time. Alex is alone in the world: the hostel has become his home and the residents and staff his family. It was moving to see their willingness not to judge and simply welcome, unlike many who had walked on by on the other side …

In Mark 10:46–52, the story of Bartimaeus the blind beggar, Jesus hears a cry for help despite being in a large crowd. He stops. He forgets the crowd who had his attention, and makes Bartimaeus the priority at that moment. And then he asks Bartimaeus what he wants. He puts Bartimaeus in charge of defining the solution, of articulating what transformation would mean to him. Jesus listens, and then he acts.

The solutions to homelessness begin with listening as Jesus did. Listening to the stories of those living that tough reality. Not judging, and trying to understand people's journeys; learning about their ambitions and aspirations and what would feel like change and a better way of life for them. Seeing others as we would want to be seen in the same situation: not as a problem but as a person, a citizen, a neighbour; someone who has as much to give as to receive. It's what is meant by unconditional love. It's not easy. It's not politically popular. It's not what would be seen as received wisdom. But it's what works best because it begins with the person not the problem. In truth, it's how we would want to be treated were we in a tough reality too.

Changing perspectives: a meditation

A bundle of clothes in a shop doorway as dusk draws in, with feet at one end and some plastic bags stuffed with everything someone owns tucked close.

A beggar outside your favourite coffeeshop.

A *Big Issue* seller outside a supermarket with limited English, a smile and a slightly desperate look of hope as you approach.

A woman with a weather-beaten face and tired eyes asking for change as you leave the takeaway.

A young man sitting beside your bus stop wrapped in a thin sleeping bag, with a dog in his lap and a sign asking for cash for a hostel.

Signs of fragile humanity.

Signs of life on the edge.

Signs of broken lives and damaged hearts.

Signs of a son, a mother, a daughter, a brother, a father, a friend, a neighbour, a colleague; lost to those who once called them so but not ceasing to still be those people.

A cry for help.

A call for hope.

A request for a little sharing of wealth.

What can we do?

Can we ever change this reality?

Can we really make a difference?

Are we not just perpetuating the system?

Will what we give be used for the purpose it was asked for?

Signs of our own struggle to love not just our neighbour but the stranger too.

We are called to love unconditionally.

We are called to love not just those who are like us but those whose world is very different to ours.

We are called to share what we have so others can have what they need.

To feed the hungry.

To give the thirsty something to drink.

To clothe the naked.

To take care of the sick.

To take the stranger into our homes.

In listening to those who are homeless,
whose tough reality we hope never to know,
and seeing them first as people, as neighbours, as fellow citizens,
let us find the strength and the courage,
the wisdom and the understanding,
to listen to your call,
to live as we are called to live,
to love as we would want to be loved,
to share what we can,
to live justly and compassionately,
whatever the cost.

Ideas for taking practical and political action

Practical action

Even if you don't want to give money or buy a *Big Issue* – acknowledge the person asking: look them in the eye with kindness even though you are not able to help financially.

If you are not sure whether to give money or food but want to do something, food is a safer bet. Ask the person if they'd like something to eat; if they say yes, ask them what they'd like to eat and get it for them. That conversation will be as important as the food itself – you will have begun the journey of listening.

Volunteer with a homelessness charity – don't worry about what skills you have, whatever you can do will be put to good use. And even if you don't want to be in the 'frontline', what you can do will be valuable and make a difference.

Make a donation either directly or by running an event to raise awareness and money. It's hugely valuable to run events not just for the money they raise but for the opportunity for a given charity to reach others they don't know and to raise the issues of perceptions about homelessness and the need for person-centred solutions.

If you can make a regular donation, however small, it will make a huge difference, and can be the way you manage feeling unable to give money directly to someone on the streets.

Donations of clothes, sleeping bags, toiletries, underwear, hats and gloves are very helpful, and they don't need to come just at Christmas. Donations of clothes for interviews are also very welcome.

Find out if there's an organisation locally who do starter packs for homes, like this one in Edinburgh: www.freshstartweb.org.uk. This makes such a difference when someone does get to the place where moving into a home is possible.

If you are feeling really ambitious – does your congregation have land and/or buildings which could be used for housing? A local housing association could provide the delivery and even the financial model. It all begins with a conversation …

Political action

Challenge politicians who support punitive policies like anti-rough-sleeping spikes on benches or clearing rough sleepers out of sight. Simple questions like 'Is that how you would want to be treated if you were in their place?' can make decision-makers very uncomfortable.

Call on politicians to support person-centred programmes, like Housing First, which have been shown to make a significant difference in the lives of those most excluded.

Support campaigns that encourage the building of more affordable housing and the alleviation of poverty. Poverty is the biggest driver of homelessness and a lack of affordable housing is the biggest barrier to finding solutions. This includes campaigns around fair rents, improved standards in private-sector housing, rent deposit schemes and alternative housing models (e.g. co-ops, self-build).

Encourage the development of prevention work such as conflict resolution workshops in schools – falling out with families is the reason most often given for young people presenting as homeless.

About the authors

Ewan Aitken is a member of the Iona Community and CEO of Cyrenians, a charity dealing with the causes and the consequences of homelessness (www.Cyrenians.scot). His royalties from this book will go directly to the work of Cyrenians.

Warren Bardsley was a human rights observer in 2008 with the World Council of Churches programme (EAPPI), serving in Jerusalem, and has visited a number of times since and led group pilgrimages. Involved in the emergence of Kairos Britain, following a week on Iona at Pentecost 2012 and the writing of *Time for Action* (a response to *A Moment of Truth*: the *'cry of faith, hope and love from the heart of Palestinian suffering'*, authored in 2009 by Palestinian church leaders, which became known as the Kairos Palestine document, and which is a call to the international community to become more critically involved in the Palestinian struggle for self-determination). Author of *It's About Time* (2015), which tells the unfolding story of Kairos Britain. Member of Friends of Sabeel and the Palestine Solidarity Campaign.

Ruth Burgess is happily retired, living in Dunblane planting and harvesting her garden and watching the antics of jackdaws and crows. Much of her working life was spent with children and young people who made her laugh, cry, question and care.

David Coleman is a member of the Iona Community, a digital artist and the Environmental Chaplain for Eco-Congregation Scotland

Roddy Cowie is an associate of the Iona Community, a lay reader in the Church of Ireland and Emeritus Professor of Psychology at Queen's, Belfast. A contributor to many Wild Goose books, he is currently working on projects concerned with self-knowledge and the relationship between Christianity and emotion.

Colin Douglas: 'I served as an Ecumenical Accompanier in Palestine/Israel for four and a half months in the summer of 2008, having previously served as locum for a couple of months at St Andrew's Scots Kirk in Jerusalem. On returning to the UK I have served on the Board of Friends of Sabeel UK for almost six years, acting as Chair of the Board for most of that time. I also served until recently as a co-opted member of the Middle East Committee of the Church of Scotland's World Mission Council.'

Elaine Gisbourne is a member of the Iona Community living in North Yorkshire. She is a Specialist Palliative Care Physiotherapist working in a hospice, and practises as a Spiritual Director. Meeting people in her role as a Street Pastor has inspired much of her writing, and she has contributed to a number of Wild Goose Publications.

Tom Gordon is a former hospice chaplain, a storyteller, a member of the Iona Community and the author of several books (Wild Goose Publications).

Janet Lees is a writer, a former Chaplain at Silcoates School in Wakefield, and is a member of the Lay Community of St Benedict. She is the author of *Word of Mouth: Using the Remembered Bible for Building Community,* and *Tell Me the Stories of Jesus: A Companion to the Remembered Bible* (Wild Goose).

Runa Mackay: 'I went to work in the Edinburgh Medical Missionary Society Hospital in Nazareth in 1955 and was there for 20 years, and then I worked for the Israeli Ministry of Health for 10 years in the Arab villages in Galilee. I 'retired' but worked with Medical Aid for Palestinians in the Occupied Territories and Lebanon for 10 years. I 'retired' again and served on the Middle East Committee of the Board of World Mission of the Church of Scotland and as a Trustee of Medical Aid for Palestinians. Nowadays, I do what I can, e.g. "sit" with the Women in Black every Saturday in Edinburgh.'

Joy Mead is a member of the Iona Community and the author of several books, including, *Words and Wonderings, A Way of Knowing, Glimpsed in Passing,* and *Walking Our Story* (Wild Goose). She occasionally leads creative writing groups, and has been involved in development education and justice and peace work.

Peter Millar is a former Warden of Iona Abbey and the author of several books, including *A Time to Mend* and *Our Hearts Still Sing* (Wild Goose).

David Osborne is a retired Anglican priest, an Iona Community member and the author of several books, including *Love for the Future* (Wild Goose).

Rosemary Power is a member of the Iona Community. She lived in Northern Ireland during the years of the Troubles, has worked on issues of social justice, preaches, and writes on spirituality, practical theology and history. She visited Palestine as a child and as an adult, when she also went to Galilee.

Eurig Scandrett: 'My first visit to Palestine was in 2010 for an education conference and I quickly saw opportunities where I could play my small part in solidarity with the Palestinian people. I discovered about the Jewish National Fund, a Zionist organisation masquerading as an environmental group, involved with ethnic cleansing in Palestine for more than 100 years; so I worked with Friends of the Earth to publish *Environmental Nakba* and raise awareness of environmental injustices against Palestinians. In 2012 I participated in San Ghan'ny, which uses singing as a non-violent method of confronting Israeli occupation in the West Bank, and in support of the boycott in Scotland. I've visited Palestine several times now: the West Bank, Palestinians in Israel and in Gaza, made many friends, learned about the oppression and the Palestinian resilience and struggle, and I've been inspired to find new ways to act in solidarity through education, through my trade union, and latterly as convenor of the Iona Community Working Group on Palestine.'

Norman Shanks is a retired Church of Scotland minister and former Leader of the Iona Community (1995-2002). He first visited Israel-Palestine in 1990 (and returned in 2017) since when he has had a close interest in justice for Palestinians, alongside other justice and peace concerns, through his membership of the Central Committee of the World Council of Churches and support for Medical Aid for Palestinians, Sabeel-Kairos UK, and other organisations. He is the author of *Iona: God's Energy – the vision and spirituality of the Iona Community* (second edition, 2009, Wild Goose Publications).

Thom M Shuman is the author of several books and downloads published by Wild Goose. He lives in Columbus, Ohio, where he serves as a transitional pastor, and is an associate member of the Iona Community.

Richard Skinner: Several collections of Richard's poetry have been published, including *Invocations* (WGP 2005) and *Colliding with God* (WGP 2017). He enjoys a collaboration with composer Nigel Walsh, being the lyricist for their musical *Bethlehem!*, as well as for several liturgical pieces and a number of songs. A former member of Cambridge University Footlights, he still occasionally writes and performs sketch-based comedy. He is a member of the Anglican parish of Central Exeter.

Isabel Smyth is a Sister of Notre Dame, with long experience in the area of interfaith relations. At present she is Secretary to the Catholic Bishops' Conference Committee for Interreligious Dialogue, Secretary to the Council of Christians and Jews and writer of the blog *www.interfaithjourneys.net*.

Jan Sutch Pickard is a member of the Iona Community and former Warden of Iona Abbey, whose previous job had involved visiting and writing about different parts of the world for the Methodist Church. She never wanted to go to 'the Land that we call Holy', but one brief visit, which moved and shocked her, became a challenge for her to learn more, reflect, pray and engage more deeply with the Israel/Palestine situation. Jan has now served twice with EAPPI, in two different villages, while home is a village on Mull. She is a storyteller, preacher and writer, and two of her poetry collections: *Between High and Low Water* and *A Pocket Full of Crumbs* (Wild Goose) contain many poems about the West Bank.

Iain Whyte is a human rights activist with long-term experience of Africa. He has done research and writing on historical slavery and abolition and has been involved with today's Anti-Slavery International. He is a retired Church of Scotland minister, a member of the Iona Community and author of several books, including *Scotland and the Abolition of Black Slavery, 1756-1838* (Edinburgh University Press).

Isabel Whyte is a Church of Scotland minister and a former Health Care Chaplain. She has been involved in conflict transformation and over the years in many justice and peace initiatives here and overseas. She is a member of the Iona Community.

Wild Goose Publications is part of the Iona Community

- An ecumenical movement of people from different walks of life and different traditions in the Christian church
- Committed to the gospel of Jesus Christ, and to following where that leads, even into the unknown
- Engaged together, and with people of goodwill across the world, in acting, reflecting and praying for justice, peace and the integrity of creation
- Convinced that the inclusive community we seek must be embodied in the community we practise

Together with our staff, we are responsible for:

- Our islands residential centres of Iona Abbey, the MacLeod Centre on Iona, and Camas Adventure Centre on the Ross of Mull

and in Glasgow:
- The administration of the Community
- Our work with young people
- Our publishing house, Wild Goose Publications
- Our association in the revitalising of worship with the Wild Goose Resource Group

The Iona Community was founded in Glasgow in 1938 by George MacLeod, minister, visionary and prophetic witness for peace, in the context of the poverty and despair of the Depression. Its original task of rebuilding the monastic ruins of Iona Abbey became a sign of hopeful rebuilding of community in Scotland and beyond. Today, we are about 280 Members, mostly in Britain, and 1500 Associate Members, with 1400 Friends worldwide. Together and apart, 'we follow the light we have, and pray for more light'.

For information on the Iona Community contact:
The Iona Community, 21 Carlton Court,
Glasgow G5 9JP, UK. Phone: 0141 429 7281
e-mail: admin@iona.org.uk; web: www.iona.org.uk

For enquiries about visiting Iona, please contact:
Iona Abbey, Isle of Iona, Argyll PA76 6SN, UK. Phone: 01681 700404
e-mail: enquiries@iona.org.uk

Wild Goose Publications, the publishing house of the Iona Community established in the Celtic Christian tradition of Saint Columba, produces books, e-books, CDs and digital downloads on:

- holistic spirituality
- social justice
- political and peace issues
- healing
- innovative approaches to worship
- song in worship, including the work of the Wild Goose Resource Group
- material for meditation and reflection

For more information:

Wild Goose Publications
The Iona Community
21 Carlton Court, Glasgow, G5 9JP, UK

Tel. +44 (0)141 429 7281
e-mail: admin@ionabooks.com

or visit our website at
www.ionabooks.com
for details of all our products and online sales